T0316581

Cambridge Elements ☰

Elements in the Politics of Development
edited by
Melani Cammett
Harvard University
Ben Ross Schneider
Massachusetts Institute of Technology

 MIT CENTER FOR INTERNATIONAL STUDIES

RETHINKING THE RESOURCE CURSE

Benjamin Smith
University of Florida
David Waldner
University of Virginia

CAMBRIDGE
UNIVERSITY PRESS

CAMBRIDGE
UNIVERSITY PRESS

University Printing House, Cambridge CB2 8BS, United Kingdom

One Liberty Plaza, 20th Floor, New York, NY 10006, USA

477 Williamstown Road, Port Melbourne, VIC 3207, Australia

314–321, 3rd Floor, Plot 3, Splendor Forum, Jasola District Centre,
New Delhi – 110025, India

79 Anson Road, #06–04/06, Singapore 079906

Cambridge University Press is part of the University of Cambridge.

It furthers the University's mission by disseminating knowledge in the pursuit of
education, learning, and research at the highest international levels of excellence.

www.cambridge.org
Information on this title: www.cambridge.org/9781108702416
DOI: 10.1017/9781108776837

© Benjamin Smith and David Waldner 2021

First published 2021

A catalogue record for this publication is available from the British Library.

ISBN 978-1-108-70241-6 Paperback
ISSN 2515-1584 (online)
ISSN 2515-1576 (print)

Rethinking the Resource Curse

Elements in the Politics of Development

DOI: 10.1017/9781108776837
First published online: March 2021

Benjamin Smith
University of Florida

David Waldner
University of Virginia

Author for correspondence: Benjamin Smith, bbsmith@ufl.edu

Abstract: This Element documents the diversity and dissensus of scholarship on the political resource curse, diagnoses its sources, and directs scholarly attention toward what the authors believe will be more fruitful avenues of future research. In the scholarship to date, there is substantial regional heterogeneity and substantial evidence denying the existence of a political resource curse. This dissensus is located in theory, measure, and research design, especially regarding measurement error and endogenous selection. The work then turns to strategies for reconnecting research on resource politics to the broader literature on democratic development. Finally, the results of the authors' own research are presented, showing that a set of historically contingent events in the Middle East and North Africa are at the root of what has been mistaken for a global political resource curse.

Keywords: resource curse, democratization, endogenous selection bias, political economy, comparative politics

ISBNs: 9781108702416 (PB), 9781108776837 (OC)
ISSNs: 2515-1584 (online), 2515-1576 (print)

Contents

1 Introduction   1

2 Exploration and Findings   5

3 Extracting Value   26

4 Refinement   42

5 The Resource Curse Reconsidered   64

6 Conclusion   77

   References   79

1 Introduction

A substantial body of scholarship developed over the past two decades argues that, conditional on the presence or magnitude of oil resources, a state is more likely to be autocratic, to have weak bureaucratic institutions, to experience civil conflict, and to suffer from economic misfortunes, especially slower rates of growth. Many hundreds of books and articles have been written about the resource curse. Michael Ross's (2001) landmark study has almost 4,000 citations, and dozens of other prominent works have been cited hundreds or thousands of times. Outside the academy, commentators on global politics and public policy frequently refer to the deleterious consequences of oil (Birdsall and Subramanian 2004; Friedman 2004, 2009).

In this Cambridge Element, we focus on the political resource curse – the claim that oil and democracy are largely antithetical to one another. We do not, and cannot, completely ignore the other elements of the resource curse literature: slower rates of economic growth, higher likelihoods of civil war, and a propensity for corruption and weak state institutions. These diverse phenomena are plausibly related to one another and so we often find scholarship considering multiple outcomes in a single study. Even scholarship that focuses directly on the political resource curse may borrow theories, concepts, methods, models, and data from scholarship that focuses on economic growth or civil war: we cannot always strictly sequester the political resource curse from other hypothesized consequences of oil wealth.

But despite occasionally trespassing into other outcomes, in what follows, we primarily discuss the large literature and derived scholarly consensus that oil wealth creates an environment inhospitable to the flourishing of democracy. The main claim we consider is that oil either degrades democracy and induces autocracy or contributes energetically to autocratic survival; or, perhaps, generates both outcomes. We concede from the beginning that an enormous wealth of scholarly material supports the claim of a political resource curse, and we exert considerable energy documenting the basis of that support. If we drill below the surface consensus that a political resource curse exists, however, we quickly hit multiple strata of debate and dissensus. While giving due weight to the reasons why scholars are convinced of the reality of a political resource curse, much of the first two sections of this Element survey various dimensions along which scholars disagree.

A first layer of debate is conceptual. The political resource curse has been defined and measured in diverse ways, not all of which are mutually consistent with one another. The political resource curse has been understood as causing regimes to become less democratic, as causing autocratic regimes whose origins were independent of oil to remain autocratic longer than non-oil autocracies, or as causing a broader phenomenon of political stability; and each of these conceptual understandings of the political resource curse can be measured in diverse ways. All of these works can be understood as supporting a claim of a political resource curse, even as they disagree, to a lesser or greater extent, with one another.

A second layer of debate is methodological. Scholars choose from a rich menu of options, starting with concepts and measures, but then moving to data sets, statistical models and assumptions, and research designs to make causal inferences from observational data. Some of these decisions appeared credible when they were first made, but, in retrospect, have been shown to yield non-credible results. Other decisions produce noncomparable findings. Consequently, while there is an enormous literature claiming to find evidence of a resource curse, these results are not necessarily cumulative and do not necessarily replicate and reinforce one another.

A third layer of debate is theoretical. There are multiple theories of the resource curse, often based on incommensurable theoretical premises but still all yielding the same testable empirical hypothesis of a negative relationship between oil wealth, however understood and measured, and democracy, however understood and measured. Even among scholars who agree that a political resource curse exists, therefore, we find substantial disagreement about how to explain it theoretically. Furthermore, several prominent scholars have presented compelling theoretical arguments that the political resource curse is conditional on a broader set of theoretical factors, such that curse-like phenomena will be observed only in specific regions of the overall parameter space.

Returning to the surface after digging through these conceptual, methodological, and theoretical strata, the initial consensus around the reality of the political resource curse appears less well established. While the bulk of published research claims to find evidence for a political resource curse, substantial and very credible analyses find either a null effect, a highly conditional effect, or, in the distinct but still important minority of cases, evidence for a resource blessing. Furthermore, even among those scholars who support the claim of a political resource curse, there are divisions over causal heterogeneity. Perhaps, as we explore further, the political resource curse exists in only specific times – after the great price hike of the 1970s, for example. Or perhaps the political resource curse becomes manifest only in specific places (and perhaps, even then, only in specific times). After all, the United States and Canada industrialized and became major economic powers in significant part because of the late-nineteenth- and early-twentieth-century influx of resource revenues, retaining democratic politics throughout. Within the developing world, decades of

Venezuelan democracy were arguably financed by oil revenues, while more recently, major oil producers and long-standing dictatorships in Indonesia and Mexico both democratized at the end of the last century.

We do not claim that there is a single "best-answer" to all of the disagreements over how to study the resource curse; neither do we claim that the existence of diverse findings and debates over concepts, methods, and theories are grounds for the theory's rejection. We comment on particular theoretical, conceptual, and methodological debates and offer suggestions; but diversity itself is no cause for concern. We do claim, however, that when one looks closely at specific claims made in the literature, and the specific methodological warrants for those claims, the conclusion that a political resource curse exists appears less unassailable than would be the case when all the diverse findings are pooled together without sufficiently discriminating appraisal.

Beyond documenting scholarly dissensus over how to study the resource curse and the findings that result, our primary goal in this Element is to engage with evidence of causal heterogeneity in the relationship of oil and politics across time and space. We also advance several new claims about this spatial and temporal heterogeneity. With reference to spatial heterogeneity, we provide evidence that the treatment effects of oil vary across at least four regions – Latin America, the Middle East, Africa, and Southeast Asia – to a greater degree than most scholarship has recognized.[1] We demonstrate substantial regional heterogeneity across the developing world since the early 1980s, with Latin American oil producers becoming democratic, Middle Eastern oil producers remaining staunchly autocratic, and distinctively mixed patterns in Africa, where most oil producers made some progress toward democracy before stalling and, in some cases, experiencing retrogression, and Southeast Asia, where the cases divide cleanly between democratic transitions and obdurate dictatorships. To explain this inter-regional diversity, we draw on institutional and coalitional theories of political regimes, presenting some evidence that the structure of autocratic institutions and the underlying coalitional basis of autocratic regimes explains why, for example, we observe autocracies thriving among Middle Eastern oil producers to a much greater degree than oil producers elsewhere.

Our two other major claims represent relatively stark deviations from the conventional wisdom about the political resource curse. First, we argue that insofar as there is a political resource curse, it is overwhelmingly a regional phenomenon restricted to the major oil-producing monarchies of the Arabian Peninsula. We argue that the small oil principalities along the eastern shore of the Arabian Peninsula represent instances of survivorship bias; when we correct

---

[1] In Section 4, we explain why we emphasize diversity in these four regions.

for this source of bias, we fail to find evidence for a political resource curse. Second, with reference to temporal heterogeneity, we advance evidence that during the recent Third Wave of democratization, oil may very well be more of a blessing than a curse, as it appears to aid democratic consolidation in at least some parts of the world.

It is not our claim that oil has absolutely no effect; we are confident that it does, as the new work we present documents. But it is not the uniform effect prevalent in the literature and it is not an effect that, in our opinion, supports a more general idea of a resource curse; if anything, the cumulative evidence we present is more consistent with the idea of relatively circumscribed enclaves of a potential resource curse and a larger region in which oil might be a modest resource blessing.

We write this Cambridge Element with the goal of documenting diversity and dissensus, diagnosing its sources, and directing scholarly attention toward what we believe will be more fruitful avenues of future research and knowledge accumulation. To achieve that goal, we have divided the main body of this Element into four major sections. We begin with a survey of the field, working chronologically to show how the study of the political resource curse has changed – conceptually, theoretically, and methodologically – over time. The first section (2 Exploration and Findings) contains relatively detailed summaries of several dozen studies of the political resource curse because we believe that any effort to evaluate a large body of scholarship, diagnose sources of dissensus, and suggest new paths forward must begin from a firm foundation: we must all have a sturdy grasp on what the field has and has not accomplished if we are to move forward. As we show in this first section, the field has undergone a long-term evolution involving several transitions to better data, models, and research designs. Despite this evolution, much work remains.

The second section (3 Extracting Value) provides our diagnosis of the strengths and weaknesses of existing scholarship. We show that the resource curse is actually a large set of different and incompatible theoretical frameworks, that advances in the conceptualization and measurement of oil wealth have rendered much of the earliest literature invalid, and that very few current studies are based on a credible research design that resolves the problem of endogeneity. We also point to the under-appreciation of two other sources of biased inferences: measurement error and endogenous selection.

The third section (4 Refinement) discusses temporal and regional heterogeneity, demonstrating strikingly different patterns of oil and democratic transition in Latin America, the Middle East, Africa, and Southeast Asia. This section then makes the case that regime outcomes in oil states are mediated by political institutions and coalitions, neither of which are fully endogenous to oil; it is our belief that focusing on institutions and coalitions can help overcome the pervasive and detrimental theoretical fragmentation that we document in the previous section.

The fourth section (5 The Resource Curse Reconsidered) presents some of our original research. We focus on the Middle East and North Africa (MENA), the global region that gave birth to theories of the rentier state and the resource curse and that provides the strongest evidence of oil-induced political dysfunction. The evidence we present, however, suggests that a set of historically contingent events in the oil-rich countries of MENA have been mistaken for a global relationship of resource wealth to political and economic dysfunction. Once we recognize that the political resource curse may be a historically contingent and highly restrictive outcome, we consider from a fresh perspective whether oil may be, at least in particular historical periods and under some conditions, the source of a pro-democratic resource blessing.

The authors of this text have literally grown up and grown older – and perhaps grown wiser – with this literature. One of us wrote his senior undergraduate thesis on the rentier state in 1984. The other, raised in Alaska and the son of its former State Geologist, began to study rentier states in 1991, and completed his doctoral dissertation on the political economy of oil in 2002. Over this long timespan, we have read the literature, argued about its findings, published our own findings, and thought long and hard about how to best move the research frontier forward. We are wise enough to know that no single study will resolve all existing debates. Our goals in this Element are as follows: to map the territory of the debates, suggest where some wrong turns might have been taken, and suggest fruitful paths forward, noting that the strength of "blessing" findings should warrant re-steering the field in a more open-minded direction. We hope the next generation of scholars will find it to be a valuable resource and guide.

2 Exploration and Findings

Research on the political resource curse stretches back five decades. Looking back over the long term, it appears that a mountain of evidence supports the theory of the political resource curse. In this section, we show that in reality, these studies constitute only the Piedmont, the elevated range of low-lying hills at the base of a mountain range. There is a large amount of evidence, but it takes the form of several piles of evidence, loosely related to one another but still not entirely consistent with each other, for each cluster of studies works with different concepts, measures, theoretical assumptions, statistical models, and research designs.

We believe it an invaluable exercise to explore these clusters of evidence in detail, to understand how much support each cluster lends to the theory but also to understand how the clusters disagree with one another. To facilitate this comparative assessment, we work through the material in three chronologically organized stages: the earliest work on the rentier state in the Middle East (roughly 1970–2000), the first decade (roughly 2000–10) of cross-national statistical research on the political resource curse (an outcome that is related to but distinct from the rentier state), and ending with the last decade of research which has featured a host of innovations – new concepts, new measures, new models, and new designs. We conclude this section by trespassing into the literature claiming a relationship between oil, corruption, and weak state institutions; we do so because corruption and weak state institutions may contribute to the erosion of democracy and because doing so brings this section full circle back to the broader concept of the rentier state with which the literature began.

We think there is an interesting trajectory of change that becomes quite evident in this section; in that sense, this section can be read as a study of how research communities develop and test ideas over time, correcting for past errors. Early cross-national statistical studies use convenient but problematic measures of oil wealth that will be shown later to lack construct validity; estimate statistical models on pooled cross-sectional, time-series data that covers a relatively brief time span and pay little attention to dynamic analysis; and are overly confident that the inclusion of covariates solves problems of endogeneity and hence pay little attention to research design. Over time, new and better measures are adopted, statistical techniques are refined, and research designs confront the problem of endogeneity more directly; but perhaps most importantly, hypotheses are refined, usually moving away from highly general and relatively vague claims to much more precise and narrow claims. Strikingly, though we do not include this material here, we have found the identical trajectory in statistical studies of the association of oil to economic growth or to civil war onset: early claims that are overly broad and lack conceptual and statistical validity are replaced by much more narrow claims based on more credible statistical models and measures. To some extent, then, the resource curse is a moving target.

The Rentier State in the Middle East, 1970–1990s

In the beginning, scholars studied the political and economic impact of oil wealth through the concept of the *rentier state*. As befitting a good narrative, the origins were relatively humble: Hossein Mahdavy's (1970) essay, "The Patterns and Problems of Economic Development in Rentier States: The Case of Iran," was published in a relatively obscure edited volume on the economic history of the Middle East since the seventh century. Mahdavy defined rentier states based on the volume of external rents, or payments from foreign individuals, companies or governments, accruing directly to the state. Oil rents were of particular interest, because oil production was largely divorced from the rest of the economy and its opportunity costs were effectively zero.

Mahdavy's paper dealt primarily with the effects of massive oil rents on Iran's economic and industrial development, but he ended with the brief but trenchant observation that because rentier states could expand their size and finance their activities without taxing their citizens, their governments enjoyed independence from their citizens, including enhanced capacity to bribe pressure groups and coerce dissidents. This theme became the foundation for a number of conceptual and theoretical amendments over the next two decades, with a handful of works codifying Mahdavy's basic insight into the pithy formulation, "no representation without taxation," inverting the more traditional claim of "no taxation without representation" (Delacroix 1980; Anderson 1987; Beblawi 1987; and Luciani 1987). These works conceptualized rentier states as "distributive or allocation states," or states whose revenues were heavily dependent on oil rents and whose primary function was thus distribution, not extraction.

While these early works were largely conceptual, with limited empirics, detailed monographic studies of Middle Eastern rentier states were being published by the end of the 1980s (Anderson 1987; Crystal 1990; Gause 1994; Vandewalle 1998; and Lowi 2009). These new works did not formally test any hypotheses and did not compare rentier states to non-rentier states, but they illustrated, through detailed case studies, the utility of the concept of the rentier state to shed light on the political implications of oil wealth. Collectively, these works shared four features. First, these works interpreted oil as contributing to *political stability*, very broadly understood. Given their sample of cases, all of which had long histories of autocratic rule, they did not claim that oil *caused* autocracy. Second, these works highlighted the key role of *coalition formation and management* mediating between oil wealth and political stability. Theda Skocpol explained (1982, 269) the 1979 Iranian Revolution, for example, by noting that the given his reliance on oil wealth, the Shah "did not rule through, or in alliance with, any independent social class." A rich vein of evidence supporting the proposition that a distributive state without the necessary social coalition would enjoy only fragile stability runs through the monographic material.

Third, these works also highlighted critical antecedent conditions that appeared to distinguish the rentier state in the Middle East: the absence of a peasantry or a class of large landlords on the Arabian Peninsula, social structures based on tribes, the "accidental" nature by which sovereign states were reluctantly formed by colonial powers, and the absence of substantial state structures prior to the mid-twentieth century. It was thus not self-evident that claims about the rentier state could be generalized beyond the contextual specificity of the Middle East. Finally, these works considered multiple phenomena to be constituted simultaneously: political stability, states with the capacity for distribution but not for extraction, and failed economic diversification as the basis for sustained growth. The next generation of scholarship would slice these phenomena into discrete dependent variables and research literatures.

The monographic literature did not, however, speak in one voice. Terry Lynn Karl (1997; see also Karl 1987) provocatively argued that Venezuela was a relatively stable democracy for many decades because of, rather than despite, its oil wealth. Venezuela's oil, she posited, "was the single most important factor in shaping the structural conditions for the breakdown of military rule, the subsequent creation of a reformist political space, and the maintenance of a *democracia pactada*" (Karl 1987, 94). Karl's analysis raises the possibility that the resource curse may be sensitive to local context, a point we develop in this Element's fourth section.

Does Oil Hinder Democracy? Studies from the First Decade

By the late 1990s, early explorations into the political and economic ramifications of oil had prepared the ground for a major expansion of research. What had started as a phenomenon generally restricted to the Middle East became – hypothetically at least – a global phenomenon, and the "antiquated" techniques of the case study would be replaced by the proliferation of data sets and quantitative models that treated economic growth, democracy, civil war, and weak state institutions as discrete consequences of oil wealth.

The study that established a discrete political resource curse as a major domain of research was Michael Ross (2001), "Does Oil Hinder Democracy?" Ross was curious whether claims from the rentier state literature could be generalized beyond the Middle East and hence adopted a pooled, cross-national statistical design, in which 113 countries were observed on an annual basis between 1971 and 1997. In a variety of models with different combinations of covariates, Ross found a statistically significant and negative coefficient on his measure of oil reliance.

Yet Ross also differed from the earlier literature in several subtle but crucial ways. First, Ross conceived of oil reliance as the share of fuel exports in GDP, not as the share of oil rents in government revenue, shifting the key concept from rentier state to rentier economy. Second, this shift from rentier state broadly understood to a narrowly defined political resource curse implied a distinctive causal story, one that relied less on the "no taxation without representation" framework and more on an "anti-modernization" account: accepting the baseline claim that rising incomes render governments more democratic, Ross argued that oil-based income caused this democratizing effect "to shrink or disappear."

Third, while the earlier rentier state literature emphasized the political stability of autocracies, Ross used the Polity scale as his measure of democracy, thereby blurring the distinction between two distinct phenomena: oil can be linked to autocracy because it enhances the survival of preexisting autocracies, whose causal origins may be completely independent of oil, or oil can be linked to autocracy because higher levels of reliance on oil exports over time can make an existing regime less democratic. Ross thus interpreted his regression coefficients as implying that rising reliance on oil exports over time would cause a state to lose points on the Polity scale (i.e., to become less democratic). Ambiguity between oil as the cause of the *type* of regime and oil as the cause of the *survival* of a regime would continue to plague the literature for the next decade, as would debate over how to best isolate cross-sectional variance (differences in oil reliance and regime scores between countries at particular points in time) from within-country variance (differences in oil reliance and regime scores in one country over time). Subsequent research by Ross (especially 2012, 2014) would make important contributions to revising these early models, measures, and methods.

Reasoning that executive discretion over natural resource rents would give incumbents a tremendous advantage in the struggle to consolidate an autocratic regime, Nathan Jensen and Leonard Wantchekon (2004) test the association between their ordinal measure of natural resource reliance (both oils and minerals) and Polity scores for forty-six African countries between 1960 and 1995. In their main finding, relative to the least dependent countries (score = 1), Polity scores in the most highly dependent countries (score = 4) were about 1.59 points lower on the twenty-one-point Polity scale. Prior to 1990, however, almost all African countries had very low Polity scores: natural resource reliance only began to make an appreciable difference in Africa after 1990, when the end of the Cold War triggered a massive movement toward democratic reforms across the continent. Yet between 1994 and 1998, they find, natural resource dependence was clearly associated with a higher probability of democratic backsliding. By distinguishing a pre-1990 and a post-1990 effect of African oil, Jensen and Wantchekon raise the possibility that contextual features across time and space may produce very specific patterns in the oil-democracy relationship.

To distinguish claims about autocratic *survival* from claims about *levels* of democracy or *types* of political regimes – claims that can sometimes be inadvertently conflated, as we have already noted – requires specific types of data and models. Reasoning that the causes of transitions to autocracy may be distinct from causes of authoritarian survival, Jay Ulfelder (2007) gathers event-history data about authoritarian regimes and tests whether oil wealth affects their rates of survival. Ulfelder codes autocratic regimes using Polity scores, and further codes each autocracy annually as undergoing a transition to democracy if a chief executive exercising effective and not just de jure authority and chosen by elections replaces one who was not. Resource dependence is measured by the share of GDP represented by resource depletion, ranging from 0 to 100 percent. The key finding relates to the hazard rate of democratic transition, the probability of the event occurring in the next time period, $t + 1$, conditional on surviving up to time t. The median autocracy with minimal resource dependence has only a minute probability of a democratic transition in any given year; resource dependence lowers this probability even further, a finding that is robust to multiple model specifications.

Finally, Silje Aslaksen (2010) published some of the earliest work using fixed-effects models that separate within-country variance from cross-sectional variance. Such models control for time-invariant, unit-level sources of heterogeneity and hence permit – at least in principle – the unambiguous interpretation of regression coefficients as unit-specific changes over time in levels of democracy subsequent to changes in levels of oil dependence. Aslaksen estimates that a 10 percent increase in the value of oil extraction as a share of GDP would be associated with a long-run decrease of approximately one-half of a point on the seven-point Freedom House index of Political Rights.

Some of the more fascinating – and surprising – evidence for the resource curse comes from the research of Ellis Goldberg, Erik Wibbels, and Eric Mvukiyehe (2008) into state-level politics in oil- and coal-rich states in the United States as far back as the late 1920s. Much scholarship would not expect to find any evidence of a resource curse in a wealthy democracy in which the oil and coal sectors are privately held and so rents do not accrue directly to the state. The authors counter (2008, 479), however, that nothing in the theory of the resource curse or its purported causal mechanisms imply that no effect should be observed in rich, industrial democracies. Accordingly, they adduce evidence that oil and coal rents are associated with lower rates of taxation and less competitive gubernatorial elections, measured by margins of victory and incumbent vote share.

A parallel stream of research formulated and tested explicitly conditional theories of oil politics that acknowledged the potential for a negative effect of oil but theorized the conditions under which oil would produce either a null effect or even a positive effect. While Benjamin Smith (2007) focused on variations in autocratic stability during the windfall oil boom of the 1970s and the subsequent oil bust from the mid-1980s through the 1990s, Thad Dunning (2008) developed a theorctical model that allowed oil to have two contrary effects on democracy, one negative and one positive, as in the case of Venezuela's oil-financed democracy. Thus, both Smith and Dunning raised the strong possibility of causal heterogeneity: rather than having a single uniform effect across time and space, oil interacted with critical antecedent variables that varied across countries in systematic ways.

Consistent with the earlier literature on the rentier state, Smith conceptualizes his dependent variable as political instability, whether regime failure, large-scale social protests, or civil war, treating instability as a binary variable coded 1 if the twenty-one-point Polity index changes by three or more points from one year to the next. Like Ross, Smith measures oil dependence using the value of oil exports as a share of GDP. Using a data set spanning the years 1960–99 and covering 107 states, Smith finds that oil wealth exerts a statistically significant negative effect on the likelihood of regime failure, "suggesting that longer-lived regimes in oil-exporting states appear to be the *representative* cases" (Smith 2007, 27, emphasis added).

Smith next considers what conditions distinguish these theory-conforming cases from "deviant" cases such as the Shah's Iran – the original rentier state – which succumbed to revolution in 1979, even as the royal treasury was flush with oil revenue. Drawing on comparative historical analysis, Smith infers that oil states are stable when they rest upon broad social coalitions and robust state institutions, and vulnerable to instability when this package of coalitions and institutions is missing. Moving further back up the causal chain, Smith next infers that variations in the strength of coalitions and state institutions derive from circumstances surrounding the initial "big push" of industrialization, or late development. Strong coalitions and state institutions result when oil revenue was scarce or nonexistent and opposition movements were powerful; in these circumstances, rulers faced little choice but to adapt their coalitions and institutions. In the absence of these political-economic incentives, weak states resting on narrow and fragile coalitions resulted and instability became a latent threat. A final set of statistical models including only the twenty-three most highly oil-dependent countries observed between 1974 and 1999 – the quarter-century of boom and bust in oil prices – and containing an interaction term between rent scarcity and opposition strength confirms this disaggregated theory of the heterogeneous effects of oil: while the interaction term is negative (reducing instability) and statistically significant, the coefficient on oil dependence, while still negative, is no longer statistically significant.

Dunning develops his theory by drawing on theories of political inequality in which the median voter under democracy is poor and prefers a high rate of taxation to fund economic redistribution while the median voter under autocracy is rich and prefers a tax rate of zero. In this model, taxation under democracy is some positive function of the level of inequality: the more total assets controlled by the rich, the more the poor will resort to redistributive taxation. Given any nontrivial level of inequality, democracy thus implies imposing large costs on the rich, who will have incentives to invest in a repressive apparatus to forestall pro-democratic movements or stage a coup against a democracy.

Within this basic set-up, oil has two sets of consequences. On the one hand, oil can motivate anti-democratic movements seeking to gain control over lucrative oil rents; on the other hand, oil rents can substitute for high levels of taxation, funding redistributive policies without imposing large costs on the rich. Observed outcomes result from a "race" between these two mechanisms. Whether the pro-democratic mechanism outweighs the anti-democratic mechanism depends on the level of inequality in the private economic sector. The higher the level of inequality in the private sector, the greater role oil income plays as a substitute for high taxes on the rich. This condition implies that without a substantial private economic sector, inequality cannot perform any pro-democratic function: oil has pro-democratic features, in other words, only in a specific region of the parameter space.

To test this theory statistically, Dunning devises a direct measure of resource rents – the quantity of funds available to finance redistributive policies – and uses the share of capital in manufacturing value-added as a measure of income inequality. Theory predicts that the coefficient on oil rent will be negative, lowering Polity scores, while the coefficient on the interaction term, oil rents times capital share, will be positive, raising Polity scores. Finding statistically significant coefficients with the predicted signs and plotting the effect of oil rents per capita over different levels of inequality clearly shows that the marginal effect of oil rents can be negative, at lower levels of inequality, or positive, at higher levels of inequality.

A final stream of research in the first decade rejects the claim of the resource curse *in toto*. Michael Herb (2005) observed that the strategy of measuring oil wealth using oil exports as a share of GDP was deeply misleading, for oil contributed to both the numerator and the denominator. Consider a counterfactual world in which Kuwait had no oil; it would, in all likelihood, be a poor autocracy, not a rich democracy. Creating a "counterfactual" data set that adjusts for both oil exports and income, Herb estimates models that do not provide consistent support for the resource curse.

The first decade of research into the existence of a global resource curse came to its end in 2011 with a powerful critique of this literature, "Do Natural Resources Fuel Authoritarianism? A Reappraisal of the Resource Curse," by Stephen Haber and Victor Menaldo. Their conclusion starkly contradicts the conventional wisdom in all of its forms, as a large series of tests finds no long-term or short-term negative relationship between oil and democracy; indeed, in many of their models, they find statistically significant *positive* coefficients on various measures of oil wealth, though the magnitudes are substantively too small to suggest an actual resource blessing.

As we have already noted, most of the statistical models are (1) pooled time-series models in which estimated coefficients are a weighted average of cross-sectional and longitudinal variance, and (2) cover a relatively brief period of time. Haber and Menaldo counter that the resource curse implies that as a country makes the transition from not producing and exporting oil to becoming an oil producer, we should observe the expected decline in that country's democracy score. Consequently, using a variety of measures, including a direct measure of fiscal reliance on oil revenues for a subset of countries and a direct measure of total oil income – neither measure being scaled to GDP – they extend their analysis to the early nineteenth century in order to observe the long-term association between oil and democracy, if it exists, for each country.

Their analysis takes three forms. First, they develop time-series plots for several dozen oil producers, allowing visual inspection of the long-term relationship of oil and democracy scores. Only eight of fifty-three countries exhibit a relationship indicative of a resource curse, with nineteen countries potentially resource blessed and twenty-six countries showing no consistent pattern of association. Second, Haber and Menaldo use standard time-series analytic tools on the eighteen countries for which they have a full series of observations of fiscal reliability: tests for stationarity, cointegration, and error-correction models. A time series is stationary if it has a time-invariant mean and variance and if the covariance between any two observations depends only on the number of lags between them. They find that both series, fiscal reliance and Polity, are nonstationary. This is critical because two nonstationary time series can appear to be correlated simply because they both trend over time. Cointegration tests consider whether two nonstationary series may still exist in a long-term equilibrium relationship, much as, in a famous illustration, a drunk walking home from a bar and her unleashed dog may both follow a random walk, but each corrects their steps to converge on the same path if they stray too far from one another. The two series are not, in the vast majority of cases, cointegrated: there is no long-term equilibrium relationship. Nonetheless, Haber and Menaldo conclude by estimating error-correction models, which are models designed to permit the estimation of both short-term effects and long-term adjustments that return the two series to equilibrium. If oil wealth shapes democracy scores, we should observe this long-term equilibrium. Yet as their models consistently show, oil and democracy unambiguously do not exist in long-term equilibrium: indeed, positive coefficients on the long-run multiplier vastly outnumber the rare negative coefficient, hinting at a resource blessing.

Haber and Menaldo conclude their analysis by switching from analysis of individual country panels to panel analysis of either all oil-reliant countries or, when using total oil income, all countries. They estimate a wide variety of models, probing for long-term relationships and short-term relationships and employing a wide variety of techniques to control for endogeneity, including fixed-effects models, instrumental variables, and a difference-in-difference estimator. Their findings are consistent across a range of models: while the coefficient on oil income is negative, that estimate is not statistically significant. If there is a political resource curse, their exhaustive search failed to find evidence for it.

Revising the Political Resource Curse, 2012–2020

The next stage of research on the political resource curse introduced several new and welcome features. Some of these developments were in response to Haber and Menaldo's powerful critique, but others would have emerged in the absence of that critique. New measures of oil dependence that were not scaled to GDP topped the list of revisions: we will discuss these in the next subsection. In addition, recognizing that levels of oil production and dependence were potentially endogenous, either to political regimes themselves or to unmeasured confounders, scholars experimented with several new research designs to minimize or eliminate bias in estimates of the causal effect of oil. We summarize these research designs and discuss their validity at greater depth in the next section.

Here we focus on three major revisions: adding temporal scope conditions, redefining the outcome variable more precisely as autocratic survival, and exploring new research designs to control for the potential endogeneity of oil to regime type. We cover each in the following three sub-sections.

Time Matters: Adding Temporal Scope Conditions

In his 2012 book and in a 2014 article coauthored with Jørgen Andersen, Michael Ross proposes that the resource curse exhibits systematic temporal heterogeneity, derived from structural changes in the international oil industry: the long century ending in 1918 when almost no countries crossed the threshold of producing significant amounts of oil (defined as US $S100 per capita); the next six decades when oil production expanded but the vast majority of rents were captured by the major oil companies; and a period beginning in approximately 1980, when, following a wave of nationalizations and price hikes, the size of government revenues grew dramatically. The key implication, Ross argues, is that Haber and Menaldo treat all three periods as causally homogeneous, when in fact, the political resource curse is a phenomenon that emerged only after the 1970s nationalization wave. Andersen and Ross test their claim of a structural break in 1980 by reestimating error-correction models and adding a term-interacting total oil income with a dummy variable for the year 1980 and finding a negative and statistically significant coefficient on this term.

Adding the scope condition that dates the origins of the political resource curse to 1980, moreover, suggests that the primary observational implication of oil wealth will be that oil-rich autocracies will have better prospects for survival than oil-deprived autocracies. As the Andersen and Ross conclude (2014, 1002), "We think – though cannot prove, in the absence of more reliable nationalization data – that when the fiscal powers of autocratically governed oil producers passed a *critical threshold in the mid to late 1970s, they became capable of withstanding the democratic wave that swept the rest of the authoritarian world in the 1980s and 1990s*" [emphasis added]. For Andersen and Ross, therefore, "the most credible version of the resource curse hypothesis ... is that when autocratic states collect a lot of oil revenues, they become less likely to transit to democracy (2014, 1017, footnote 6).

Consequently, Andersen and Ross categorically reject Haber and Menaldo's use of within-country, time-series panels to test the theory of the resource curse; given their new emphasis on the failure of oil states to make a transition to democracy after 1980, a within-country research design misidentifies the nature of the control group. "Haber and Menaldo," they aver, "compare countries 'treated' with natural resource wealth to themselves over time, instead of comparing them with countries without resource wealth ... If they compared the resource-producing countries with ... the nonresource countries, which happened to grow more democratic after the 1970s ... they would have observed that the 'resource treatment,' and in particular oil, has had a profound antidemocratic effect" (Andersen and Ross 2014, 1004). Ross (2012) estimates logistic regression models of the probability of a democratic transition and finds evidence consistent with this new version of the political resource curse hypothesis.

Redefining the Resource Curse as Autocratic Survival

Over the past decade or so, research on oil, autocratic survival, and even leadership survival has flourished. David Wiens, Paul Poast, and William Clark (2014) agree with Ross that the theory of the resource curse implies only autocratic survival, not the erosion or subversion of democracy, because democracies impose institutional constraints on elected leaders. It is therefore a profound conceptual mistake, they argue, to test the resource curse using measures of levels of democracy; the proper specification is a binary variable to test the hypothesis that an increase in resource dependence decreases the likelihood of a democratic transition at time t given that a country is autocratic at time $t-1$. Whereas Ulfelder and Ross tested this hypothesis on data sets that contained only autocracies, Wiens, Poast, and Clark estimate dynamic logit models to simultaneously estimate the effects of oil on both types of regime, interacting a continuous measure of resource dependence with an indicator of regime type. They find that resource dependence decreases the probability of a democratic transition but has no effect on existing democracies.

Joseph Wright, Erika Frantz, and Barbara Geddes (2015) test whether oil influences two distinct types of transitions following autocratic breakdown: either a transition from autocracy to democracy or a transition from one autocratic regime to a different autocratic regime, such as the Iranian Revolution which overthrew a monarchy and replaced it with a theocracy. Using a new dataset that distinguishes distinct autocratic regimes from one another, they estimate models of oil and autocratic regime survival that cleverly allow for both within-country effects (a unit fixed effect) and cross-sectional effects. They estimate one coefficient on the *within-country* variation in oil wealth (an annual measure of the deviation of oil wealth from the mean level of oil wealth for that country, $O_{i,t-1}-\overline{O}_i$, representing the effect of marginal changes in a country's oil level) and a second coefficient on the mean level of oil for each country, $\overline{O}_i$, to model whether average levels of oil wealth that vary across countries have a separate effect. Furthermore, to allow for country-specific intercepts, they include the average regime-change score for each country, proposing that "Unobserved factors that vary by country and may also be correlated with the level of oil rents and the latent propensity for regime collapse should be captured in the unit means for regime change" (2015, 295).

Looking only at democratic transitions, between-country differences in mean levels of oil wealth have a negative and statistically significant relationship with the probability of a transition; within-country differences (the marginal effect of changes in a given country's oil wealth) is negative but far from statistically significant. The negative between-country relationship is consistent with the bulk of the literature; the absence of statistical evidence for a within-country negative relationship, in contrast, is consistent with Haber and Menaldo's rejection of the resource curse. Turning to autocratic-to-autocratic transitions, the findings are reversed: increasing oil wealth within individual dictatorships over time deters the likelihood of transitions to new dictatorships while between-country differences have no statistically significant effect. It is puzzling why within-country variance seems to decrease the likelihood of intra-authoritarian transitions but has no effect on democratic transitions that can be distinguished statistically from zero. As the authors conclude, "We see understanding whether the between-country correlation reflects characteristic and relatively stable institutional changes caused by resource wealth or simply identifies preexisting conditions as a next step in this research agenda" (Geddes et al. 2015, 304).

Viola Lucas and Thomas Richter (2016) replicate the Wright, Frantz, and Geddes models in all respects, but substitute a new measure of state hydrocarbon rents culled from the Global State Revenues and Expenditure dataset, based on newly released IMF documents, containing 39 different indicators of state finances for 161 countries between 1946 and 2006. Their models find no statistically significant relationship between oil rents and the probability of an autocracy-to-autocracy transition, using either the within-country variation in marginal levels of oil rents or the between-country variation in mean oil rents. Both measures of oil rents, within-country and between-country, on the other hand, have a statistically significant and negative relationship with the probability of democratic transitions. These findings directly challenge those of Wright, Frantz, and Geddes; but a rejoinder by Wright and Frantz (2017) points to systematic measurement error as a likely cause of these results.

Christian Houle (2019) maintains the distinction between autocratic failure and democratic transition, but argues for a sequenced approach: rather than viewing new autocracies and democratic transitions as alternative outcomes, he first models autocratic failures as a single category and then models the probability of a democratic transition versus intra-authoritarian transition, conditional on prior autocratic failure. Operationally, this means that while Wright, Frantz, and Geddes estimate the probability of a transition to democracy using all country-years, Houle's conditional approach models democratic transitions only for the smaller subset of countries that have recently experienced autocratic failure. Conceptually, because Houle must model failure as distinct from any type of transition, he considers a broad range of instances of irregular leader removal to constitute authoritarian failures. Using this distinct measure of autocratic failure, Houle concludes that oil has no effect on the probability of autocratic failure, but a large and negative effect on the probability of a democratic transition conditional on the prior autocratic failure.

In direct contrast to Houle's findings, Crespo Cuaresma, Harald Oberhofer, and Paul Raschky (2011) estimate models of the effects of oil rents on the survival of individual dictators. They find that while crude oil reserves increase the duration of dictators, increases in world oil prices increase the probability of a successful coup d'etat, breaking the equilibrium between the dictator and his rivals. Similarly, Jørgen Andersen and Silje Aslaksen (2013) model the survival of political parties, creating a binary-dependent variable for political change in which the chief executive belongs to a different party than last year's executive. Conditioning their analysis on three categories of initial political institutions based on Polity indicators, they find that access to oil rents affects political survival, but primarily in nondemocracies.

Finally, to complete this cycle of studies on oil and political survival, Kevin Morrison (2009) finds that all categories of nontax revenue, including oil rents, lower the taxation of elites in democracies, increase social spending in dictatorships, and boost political stability in *both* types of regime, with stability measured by the Polity binary variable coded as 1 if the Polity score has changed by three or more points since the previous year. Far from being disadvantageous for democracies, as so many have argued, Morrison leaves us with another tantalizing clue that oil and oil-like revenues may be more blessing than curse.

The works just surveyed differ from one another theoretically, conceptually, and methodologically, and their findings are not fully consistent with one another; but they all provide *some* evidence that oil matters for autocratic survival without harming existing democracies. Victor Menaldo (2012, 2016), on the other hand, provides strong evidence against this conclusion. Already a skeptic of the resource curse, Menaldo considers the *type* of autocratic regime – monarchies versus republics – to be a crucial omitted variable. Focusing exclusively on the Middle East and North Africa, Menaldo argues that the region's monarchies have developed distinctive political cultures that create focal points for elite coordination and hence radically diminish threats of political instability, even as oil income declined after the 1970s boom. Menaldo estimates models of the effect of total per capita fuel income on the probability of revolution, a measure defined as "any illegal or forced change in the top government elite, any attempt at such a change, or any successful or unsuccessful armed rebellion whose aim is independence from the central government" (2015, 302). Estimating Cox proportional hazards survival models, Menaldo finds a negative and significant association of oil to revolution in models with no covariates; but the addition of a dummy variable for monarchy (as well as other covariates) reduces the coefficient of oil by more than half and renders it statistically insignificant; the coefficient on monarchy, on the other hand, is negative and statistically significant. Within the Middle East, the region that gave birth to the idea of the rentier state, the effect of oil basically disappears when we take the distinctiveness of monarchies into account. We return to the issue of regional heterogeneity and other contextual factors, including types of autocratic regimes, in Section 4.

Searching for Exogeneity: New Research Designs

Finally, we turn to questions of research design and causal identification. To be an oil producer requires location atop an oil-bearing geologic structure from which oil can be extracted at a profit; in principle, oil revenues fall like "manna from heaven." Yet there are also political decisions that can influence the flow of oil rents to a government, including decisions about exploration that may be influenced by available technology, local human capital formation, and forecasts of future political stability, as well as decisions about rates of extraction that may be influenced by rulers' discount rates that may themselves be conditioned on type of political regime, strength of state institutions, or other political institutions or contextual factors that might influence democracy (Haber 2008, Dunning 2010, and Menaldo 2015 productively explore these possibilities). Estimating the causal effect of oil thus requires research designs to mitigate these sources of bias.

Several studies have sought to identify exogenous variation in oil abundance or dependence using instrumental variables. These are variables that predict oil income but are not associated with political regimes by any causal pathway that does not pass through oil income. Instrumental variables can take the form of exogenous determinants of the supply of oil or the price of oil. Kevin Tsui (2011) proposes oil endowment, an estimate of the total oil in place as determined by statistical inference based on geological characteristics and information about cumulative discoveries, as an exogenous instrument to predict the peak amount of total oil discovered, which may be endogenous to political institutions. Because oil endowment and peak volume of discovered oil are both constants, Tsui estimates a cross-sectional design in which the dependent variable is the decennial average Polity score three decades after peak discovery and includes as a regressor the decennial average Polity score one decade prior to peak discovery. His models estimate that a discovery of 100 billion barrels of oil (a total discovery equal to those of Iraq, one of the most oil-abundant countries in the world) will, over the thirty years following peak discovery, be associated with a Polity score between 10 percent and 15 percent lower (approximately two to three points on the twenty-one-point Polity scale) than a country with no oil wealth. Travis Cassidy (2019) uses a potentially superior instrument, information on sedimentary basins in which hydrocarbons can form. In a purely cross-sectional design, Cassidy estimates that a one-standard deviation increase in the predicted value of the logged average per capita level of oil production is associated with a reduced Polity score of about one-half of a standard deviation – about 0.16 on the normalized 0–1 scale.

In contrast, Kristopher Ramsay (2011) proposes that out-of-region natural disasters that disrupt oil production and distribution cause exogenous price hikes and increase oil income, independent of any action taken by the government or possibly omitted variables. Restricting the instrument to "out-of-region" disasters, ensures that there is no conceivable direct link between the natural disaster itself and the outcome variable. Estimating a data set covering forty-eight "nonnegligible" oil producers for the years 1968–2002, Ramsay estimates that a 3 percent increase in oil income generated exclusively by out-of-region, disaster-induced price hikes is associated with a two-point reduction in the country's Polity score in the short term.

Other instrumental-variable designs, however, have reached contradictory conclusions. Romain Wacziarg (2012, 642) argues that while production levels may be endogenous, "Oil prices are determined by world markets and are less likely to be endogenously affected by a single producer's domestic circumstances, particularly at the one-year frequency employed by this paper." Wacziarg constructs two time-series spanning the years 1960–2007, one for average crude oil prices and one for Polity scores of major oil producers: each is nonstationary and they are not cointegrated. Taking the first differences of the series to produce stationary series of changes in prices and levels of democracy, Wacziarg finds a positive and statistically significant coefficient of world oil prices on average Polity scores, a finding that is robust to multiple specifications.

Sarah Brooks and Marcus Kurtz (2016) echo this finding. Because the amount of oil that is detected and extracted is a function of investment, oil field management, and technology (Wright and Czelusta 2007), they hypothesize that oil revenue (net of subsoil endowments) should respond positively to the level of industrialization and the stock of human capital, a hypothesis borne out by regression analysis of oil income as the dependent variable. Development, in turn, is subject to regional diffusion effects. In a variety of models that control for these diffusion effects, including instrumenting oil income on the ratio of proven reserves to physical area, fixed-effects models, and a measure of oil income "predicted" by the level of industrialization, they find coefficients with small but positive and statistically significant coefficients.

Reasoning that most efforts to find a valid instrument for oil discoveries, endowments, and production will fail, Yu-Ming Liou and Paul Musgrave (2014) present an analysis using the synthetic control which systematically constructs an optimal control unit for a treated country as the weighted average of attributes from a set of appropriate "donor" countries (Abadie, Diamond, and Hainmuller 2015). Liou and Musgrave center their analysis on the 1973–4 oil price hike, prior to which several countries were "latent" oil producers that began to produce substantial amounts of oil in response to higher prices. For the decade prior to the oil boom, which Liou and Musgrave argue convincingly was exogenous relative to their treated units, each country has a regime history that, by design of the method, closely tracks the regime history of the composite control unit; we can then observe how levels of democracy change in the decade following the boom, with the synthetic control representing the counterfactual outcome of no oil production. Any deviations between the post-treatment regime history of the treated and control units can then be tested for statistical significance using placebo tests.

Five of the seven treated cases – Trinidad, Algeria, Gabon, Indonesia, and Nigeria – had democracy scores in the mid-1980s that were statistically indistinguishable from their counterfactuals: as far as we can tell, the massive oil windfalls had no effect at all on their democracy scores. Only Ecuador and Mexico evince outcomes that can be statistically distinguished from zero, with Ecuador having a higher-than-predicted democracy score and Mexico a lower-than-predicted democracy score. Liou and Musgrave (2014, 1601) conclude that while their results may not be an absolute "knockout blow" against the resource curse, evidence for an anti-democratic effect of oil cannot be consistently found for a carefully curated and analyzed set of cases.

Oil and State Institutions

We think it important to end this overview with studies of oil and state institutions. Many claims about the resource curse are in fact conditional on weak state institutions: oil might be compatible with economic growth, civil concord, and even democracy if it is exploited by an institutionally strong state. Yet such a happy outcome would not be possible if oil rents *cause* weak state institutions.

The genesis of the claim that oil rents weaken states can be found in Mahdavy's original 1970 paper, in which he proposed that "not having developed an effective administration machinery for the purposes of taxation, the governments of Rentier States may suffer from inefficiency in any field of activity that requires extensive organizational inputs" (Mahdavy 1970, 467). Besley and Persson (2010) provide a formal model that demonstrates this proposition. Note, however, that oil and state weakness may be associated in three different ways: the onset of substantial oil revenues may (1) weaken the state absolutely, eliminating capacity that existed in the pre-oil era; (2) retain existing capacity but remain in a low-capacity equilibrium, extending the institutional status quo and preempting future institutional development; or (3) reduce the rate of capacity-building institutional change, such that oil states develop state capacity but more slowly relative to otherwise similar non-oil states.

Some of the early case-study research on oil and state strength exacerbated this ambiguity. Terry Lynn Karl's influential work on the Venezuelan petro-state made plausible arguments that states relying for their revenues on external rents will exhibit broad structural similarities that distinguish them sharply from the coherent and highly institutionalized bureaucracies of Western Europe. Yet Karl (1997) makes inconsistent claims about the oil-state nexus, first arguing that oil rents "expand the state's jurisdiction while simultaneously *weakening* its authority" (p. 15), but later arguing that under the influence of oil rents, the state expanded but "did not develop political authority at the same pace … its institutional evolution proceeded far more slowly and unevenly" (p. 59–60). Karl's claims, moreover, might be undermined by comparing pre-oil Venezuela to the post-oil state. In the pre-oil period, "The weak legacy of state building predated the exploitation of petroleum," Karl observes, such that on the eve of oil exploration, "Venezuela continued to fall behind most of the continent in state building as it entered the modern era" (1997, 74, 75). If Venezuela was not developing a strong state, even by Latin American standards, prior to the large-scale exploitation of oil, then we have no reason to accept the counterfactual that oil production prevented an inevitable trajectory of state building that would have occurred in an oil-free Venezuela.

Kiren Chaudhry's study of oil and the state in Saudi Arabia seemingly makes a stronger case that the oil windfall of the 1970s led to the systematic dismantling of much of the Saudi state and its extractive capacity. Chaudhry goes to considerable lengths to support her claim that in the pre-oil era, beginning in the 1920s, "the quest for ever increasing tax revenues generated an extensive and increasingly efficient extractive and regulatory bureaucracy" (Chaudhry 1997, 47). As Saudi Arabia slowly entered the oil age in the 1950s, moreover, increasing oil revenues strengthened "the extractive efforts of the Saudi state in some ways while allowing it to withdraw from particularly costly and destabilizing forms of taxation" (p. 76). This strengthening of the state occurred even though oil rents extracted from ARAMCO and others accounted for the vast proportion of state revenues, with domestic taxation chipping in only seven percent in the 1960s (p. 83). As long as oil revenues remained "moderate"

(p. 84), Saudi state-building conformed to "the broadest sequencing patterns of state-making in early modern Europe" (p. 98). Yet the oil boom of the 1970s did not merely suspend further development of the Saudi Leviathan: rather, by the end of the decade, "hardly a vestige of this pre-boom institutional construct remained. In a mere decade, the regulatory and extractive capabilities of the Saudi state had all but vanished" (p. 140).

If Chaudhry's account is true, then pre-oil Saudi Arabia is a true outlier: we are not aware of any other scholarship on any instance of post-colonial state building that makes such a strong claim of a late-developing state recapitulating the European state-building experience to the extent that Chaudhry claims for Saudi Arabia; most non-oil states are still, on average, relatively weak states, reliant for decades on external support to substitute for internal state capacity. Furthermore, other scholars have questioned whether Saudi Arabia is truly an outlier at successful and autonomous pre-oil state building. Both Robert Vitalis (1999, 2009) and Steffen Hertog (2010), among others, have demonstrated that foreign capital, foreign advisers, and expatriate civil servants were more central to the Saudi experience than Chaudhry acknowledges. Hertog also demonstrates that Saudi rulers began the initial construction of modern state institutions only in the late 1950s and 1960s, when "rising oil income allowed for lateral, sprawling growth of bureaucracies, leading to the evolution of small "statelets within the state," each under the control of a prince using the state to dispense patronage" (2010, 16) If the Saudi state was not built as a set of strong and autonomous institutions prior to the 1970s oil boom, then the claim that the onset of massive oil wealth led to the dismantling of state capacity lacks credibility.

More recently, scholars have estimated cross-national statistical models to investigate whether oil rents have a negative effect on indicators of state strength. In some studies, the dependent variable is conceptualized as the quality of governance using indicators of policy outcomes, such as the protection of private property, the maintenance of a policy environment conducive to investment, or the absence of bureaucratic regulation. Others study the extent of corruption, often relying on expert surveys about the prevalence of bribery or other indicators of malgovernance. For example, Rabah Arezki and Marcus Brückner (2011) analyzed panel data for thirty oil-exporting countries between 1992 and 2005. Measuring corruption with a six-point scale produced by a private firm, Political Risk Services, they estimate fixed-effects models and find that a unit standard deviation increase in oil export value is associated with an increase of about a third of a standard deviation in the corruption index. This finding is broadly consistent with a similar study by Mette Anthonsen, Åsa Löfgren, Klaus Nilsson, and Joakim Westerlund (2012).

In a very intriguing study, Pedro Vicente (2010) studies the announced discovery of oil reserves in Sao Tome and Principe, so the treatment is information about future oil revenues, not the availability and control over these revenues. Vicente uses Cape Verde as an appropriate comparator to estimate various difference-in-difference estimators, distinguishing the pre-oil period from the post-treatment period and using Cape Verde as the proxy for a counterfactual outcome without oil. Vicente implements a unique household survey about the perception of the importance of political connections to the availability of public goods and services and finds a pronounced effect for oil.

Despite these findings, there are conceptual, theoretical, and methodological reasons for a prudent skepticism. Marcus Kurtz and Andrew Schrank (2007) raise persuasive objections to the use of standard cross-national measures of good governance as proxy measures of state capability. Most of these indicators describe outcomes, not capabilities; furthermore, these measures of outcomes are derived from normative evaluations of what states should and should not do, raising the large risk that subjective agreement with a policy is being conflated with an objective measure of capability. Thus, states that impose regulations to protect, for example, public health, the environment, or critical economic sectors may be perceived to be corrupt, ineffective, overly burdensome, and growth inhibiting. Daniel Treisman (2007) makes analogous criticisms of expert-based measures of corruption, such as those reported by Political Risk Services. Indeed, insofar as respondents have some prior beliefs about the resource curse (which may be shaped by this very research program), their perceptions may be unduly influenced by the theory, making these measures a poor test of it.

The theory that oil rents impair political institutions suffers from a core theoretical problem as well, as several authors have pointed out. Consider a newly independent country, with an underdeveloped economy and weak political institutions. In rapid manner, however, the country enjoys a massive boost to its income through windfall oil profits, which in many cases act as "manna from heaven," as Alexeev and Conrad (2009) put it. Michael Ross (2012) cleverly refers to this problem as the "Beverly Hillbillies Fallacy," for when we control for income in our cross-national statistical models, we compare newly rich but institutionally weak countries to rich non-oil countries, a peer group that, almost by definition, will have strong state institutions. Oil appears to be dysfunctional for political institutions because we are making the wrong comparisons. As Paine (2016) pointed out, the problem is that while our statistical models treat income as a confounding variable and hence causally prior to oil rents, in fact income is an effect of oil wealth and hence should be treated as a mediator. Failure to properly construct the statistical model thus leads to post-treatment bias. Ryan Kennedy and Lydia Tiede (2013) correct for the endogeneity of income to oil and conclude that the evidence for a *positive* effect of oil rents on governance appears relatively strong. Kennedy and Tiede thus take us back to Smith's (2007) argument that, under certain conditions, rulers may use their oil wealth to enhance state building.

Pauline Jones Luong and Erika Weinthal (2001, 2010) also conclude that the effects of oil on political institutions are mediated by the ownership structure of the oil industry. They draw on the experiences of the five oil-rich former Soviet republics between the collapse of the USSR in 1991 and 2005. Different ownership structures generated distinct primary actors, distinct modes of business–state relationships, distinct incentives for building strong institutions, and hence, distinct institutional outcomes, ranging from weak to hybrid to strong. In short, Jones Luong and Weinthal argue, institutional choice regarding ownership – which is in part driven by societal conflicts over distribution and which we echo is central in the sections that follow – shapes oil's impact, which subsequently shapes other political institutions and development trajectories. Moreover, they highlight another dynamic to which we will return: changes in the structure of the world oil market generate substantial heterogeneity in the incentives that oil wealth creates depending on which point in recent time we are focused on.

Conclusion

There is a substantial body of research that claims to demonstrate the existence of a political resource curse. Yet we should approach this literature cautiously and prudently before determining that there is a broad consensus. First, the three periods we have looked at feature relatively sharp discontinuities from one another, with two major transitions: from qualitative studies of the rentier state to cross-national statistical models of an ill-defined political resource curse and then a second transition to the most recent studies using superior measures, models, and research designs. Second, there is substantial variation within the literature, including dissensus about the very nature of the dependent variable, with some scholarship claiming that oil reduces the level of democracy, some scholarship claiming that oil reduces the probability of a transition from autocracy to dictatorship, and some scholarship arguing both. A set of studies can all be rightly characterized as finding a negative relationship between oil and democracy yet still be characterized by large conceptual, methodological and theoretical differences that do not all comport with one another. Third, not all of the research is based on uniformly credible statistical models and research designs. Finally, there are substantial literatures that suggest either a conditional relationship, such that the effect of oil can "flip" from negative to positive or from negative to a null effect based on specific values of the parameter space; and there are substantial literatures that find no effect at all. Much work thus remains to be done. The following section begins this work by enumerating the sources of such heterogenous findings and providing a more critical evaluation of the theories, measures, models, and designs used to test the theory of the political resource curse.

3 Extracting Value

In a meta-analysis of 29 published studies of the political resource curse reporting 246 estimated coefficients, Anar Ahmadov (2014) reports that 86 percent of statistically significant findings report a negative coefficient and just 14 percent report a positive coefficient. Yet hypothesis tests of 1 in 5 of the 246 estimated coefficients fail to reject the null hypothesis and thus are not indicative of a statistically significant relationship. We thus have positive findings, negative findings, and null findings. As Ahmadov judiciously concludes, "the debate cannot be resolved based on 'vote counting' as it would ignore, rather than incorporate, these usually substantiated decisions" (2014, 1239).

In this section, we attribute the heterogeneity of findings to theoretical debates, disagreements about measures and concepts, and varieties of research designs. We do not claim that reviewing this material allows us to definitively adjudicate disputes over the resource curse, but we think it will still be valuable to define with some precision specific areas of disagreement. We aim to expose the "high-value" areas of dispute in which scholars may be provoked into rethinking their positions and refining subsequent work by making better choices – or at least better and more transparently justified choices. We conclude this section with discussion of measurement bias and endogenous selection bias; neither of these two sources of bias has been considered systematically by the existing literature.

Rival Theories of the Political Resource Curse

It is somewhat customary to refer to "the" theory of the resource course, with the tacit understanding that the theory refers to a negative relationship between oil and democracy. But on this very broad and rather shallow understanding, scholars have in fact generated a well-populated family of loosely related theories and intra-family disputes. Theories of the political resource curse are propositions about how oil might cause countries to deviate from a baseline model of democratic development representing a counterfactual state of the world in which a given oil producer is deprived of its oil wealth. These baseline models are in turn derived from more encompassing theories of democracy. We identify four distinct versions of this baseline theory of democracy in the existing literature: anti-modernization theory, a fiscal theory of democracy, redistributive conflict theory, and elite-conflict theory.

Michael Ross (2001, 325) offers a clear statement of what is perhaps the most widespread interpretation of the resource curse: "Many studies show that when incomes rise, governments tend to become more democratic. Yet some scholars imply there is an exception to this rule: if rising incomes can be traced to a country's oil wealth, this democratizing effect will shrink or disappear." This baseline theoretical expectation informs how Ross interprets (2001, 342) his regression coefficients: as reflecting a change in levels over time within an individual country, as "a single standard deviation rise in the *Oil* variable produces a .49 drop in the 0–10 democracy index over the five-year period ... A state that is highly reliant on oil exports ... would lose 1.5 points on the democracy scale due to its oil wealth alone." Most scholarship tacitly agrees with this position by adding national income – arguably a post-treatment variable, not a proper control variable representing a common cause of treatment and outcome – to regression models with the expectation that it will be positively signed.

In subsequent work, however, Ross (2012, 67–71) argues for a revised theory of the resource curse, a "fiscal theory of democracy" that, as we have seen, becomes operative only after 1980, when changes in the structure of the international oil industry shifted the distribution of oil income between international companies and states. The revised theory presupposes an incumbent autocrat secure in office unless citizens "resort to strikes, demonstrations, or riots to force a leader from power." Citizens act collectively or acquiesce to autocracy based upon their perception of how government policies affect their incomes, acting to replace governments that either tax too much or spend too little on public goods. In autocracies with oil, moreover, citizens' utility is based on the government's spending-to-revenue ratio; above some threshold of spending on public services as a share of oil revenues, citizens do not demand democracy; below the relevant threshold of benefits to revenues, citizens could engage in pro-democratic uprisings. Thus, rulers can boost their popularity and remain as incumbent autocrats by (1) spending on public benefits; and (2) concealing the true size of their oil revenues so that public benefits appear to be above the rebellion threshold. Ross (2012, 69) thus concludes that, "While autocracies without oil gradually become democratic, autocracies with oil can remain autocratic."

In contrast, theories of redistributive conflict model democracy as conflict between social classes, abstractly portrayed as rich versus poor, in which democracies are costly to the rich because the median voter, poor by definition, will tax the rich to pay for redistributive social spending, with the level of redistributive taxation a positive function of the level of income inequality. The general expectation is that democracy is a feasible outcome at relatively low levels of inequality, and that the prospects for democracy decline with rising levels of inequality. There is some disagreement, however, about the predicted outcome at the highest levels of inequality. While oil may introduce destabilizing conflict as groups seek to capture power and hence lucrative rents, oil rents may also finance public spending without taxing the rich, alleviating the demand for an anti-democratic coup and raising the acceptability of democracy for the rich. Thus, when inequality and hence the demand for state support for the poor is relatively elevated, oil-rich democracies may survive longer than resource-deprived democracies because they can satisfy the poor without imposing intolerable costs on the rich.

Finally, elite-conflict theory primarily studies the determinants of autocratic stability. In these models, the key dynamic is latent conflict between incumbent autocratic elites and potential rival elite groups who might wish to install an autocracy under their own control. Citizens play a negligible role in most of these models; Houle (2019, 407), for example, argues that pro-democracy movements play almost no role in forcing dictators to initiate political reforms. Autocracies survive, rather, when the incumbent ruling group devises instruments for preempting the threat of violent overthrow by rival elites: oil wealth is thus highly functional to autocratic survival because it can be used to maintain elite cohesion and hence minimize threats to autocratic survival. A theory that is premised on inter-elite conflict and that denies substantial citizen involvement is, barring heroic efforts at synthesis, incompatible with either a fiscal theory of democracy or a redistributive conflict theory.

Distinct theories have distinct observable implications. Anti-modernization theory generates an expectation of an over-time relationship between levels of oil wealth and democracy scores among all countries, democracies and dictatorships. Ross's fiscal theory of democracy, on the other hand, implies a contrast between oil-rich and oil-poor autocracies, with the latter having a higher probability of transition to democracy after 1980.

Elite-conflict theory also works with a dataset of all autocracies and estimates the probability of a transition; however, these theories allow for two types of transitions, a transition to a new autocracy and a democratic transition. Therefore, testing these theories requires a specific data set that distinguishes intra-authoritarian transitions, and also requires crafting specific statistical models to test the two possible transition paths.

Fundamental disagreements about what types of observations are implied by the "theory" of the resource curse are inevitable. For Haber and Menaldo (2011), the resource curse is a theory about a dynamic process that generates changes within a country over time: a country whose reliance on natural resources increases over time should experience, with perhaps a modest time lag, correspondingly decreasing changes in its level of democracy. Andersen and Ross (2014, 1004) unequivocally disagree. The theory of the resource curse, they object, does not imply "that *changes* in resource reliance led to *changes* in Polity scores . . . the resource curse is not a theory about changes, but a theory about levels." Specifically, it is a theory about "why the oil and nonoil states diverged after the 1970s." Given this presupposition about what the theory implies, Andersen and Ross utterly reject the Haber-Menaldo finding of a potential resource blessing because, they aver, it is based on flawed reasoning. Haber and Menaldo's study "can tell us the *conditional probability* that a country with more (or less) resource wealth will democratize; the important question, however, is whether resource-rich countries are more likely, or less likely, to democratize than similar countries without resource wealth" (Andersen and Ross 2014, 1003–1004, emphasis in original).

We believe that these two claims are not as incompatible as Anderson and Ross suggest. We also believe that it is not self-evident whether one version of the question (why did non-oil countries have a higher probability of transition to democracy after 1980 than oil countries) is "more important" than an alternative version of the question (as a country increases or decreases its reliance on oil revenues, does it become correspondingly less or more democratic?) Either version of the question is fully compatible with at least one version of the theory of the resource curse. After all, a large body of literature investigates the relationship of levels of resource wealth to levels of democracy, and much of that literature finds that there is a relationship. Furthermore, even if we confine the research agenda to the effects of oil on autocratic stability, scholars can still approach the question from a wide variety of angles and reach some very different conclusions.

Finally, beneath the level of baseline theories of democracy that set expectations about how oil is likely to cause distinct trajectories, there is what we call a "standard model" of the resource curse. The standard model is a narrow perspective on oil: without asking big questions about democracy, the standard model simply posits a modal political agent – usually an incumbent leader – with and without oil, positing that oil will change that agent's behavior in ways that are largely detrimental to democracy. Yet even at this level, there are important sources of variation. First, the relevant political leaders may exist in a democracy or in a dictatorship, so that the threat posed by oil is to either erode or eliminate an existing democracy or to prevent a democratic transition. Second, oil can affect a leader's incentives, capabilities, or both. The existence of oil in a democracy transforms a leader with pro-democratic preferences into a leader who prefers autocracy and its attendant monopolistic control over lucrative oil rents. Alternatively, the existence of oil in a dictatorship may give a leader, who would otherwise be susceptible to pro-democratic pressure, greater capacity to resist pro-democratic movements or to co-opt citizens into accepting the autocratic status quo. Finally, these models can differ in terms of their posited mechanisms: rulers might employ oil rents as carrots, as sticks, or in different combinations of carrots and sticks aimed at different segments of the population.

In short, there is substantial variation in how we conceive of the resource curse; differences in our theoretical conceptions can, in many ways, shape the way we construe our research projects. Different theoretical starting points, moreover, may motivate the selection of different concepts and indicators.

Concepts and Measures

Disagreements over measurement are usually viewed exclusively as debates over indicators: what are the most appropriate measures of oil wealth, the independent variable, and of democracy, the dependent variable? Theories of the political resource curse relate cognate constructs like "oil wealth," "oil rents," or "oil reliance" to the construct "political regime." These are background concepts that embody a broad constellation of meanings; empirical research requires first the formulation of a systematized concept from among the broad meanings and second the development of one or more indicators of the systematized concept that can be applied to individual cases to score or code the case. Because scholars execute these tasks differently, variations in concepts and indicators may in turn contribute to the heterogeneity of findings.

We can conceive of oil having very different types of effects on a political regime. Either oil can catalyze a transition from one regime type to the other – typically, of course, from democracy to dictatorship, but other types of transitions are possible – or oil can have no effect on the initial establishment of a regime but can bolster the stability of a given regime that has been exogenously determined; of course in principle oil could have both effects. And none of these dynamics involving a binary regime schema tell us much about the large number of "hybrid" regimes that fit neither category neatly.

Next, consider oil wealth as a concept and as a measure, keeping in mind the distinction between oil as a material substance and quantifiable commodity and oil "rents" as a theoretical construct that operates through some mechanism or mechanisms to shape the political calculations and actions of leaders, citizens, or both. The construct of oil rent or oil wealth shares this binary nature: oil as a commodity can provide resources that enhance capability, but information about oil can independently shape incentives. In fact, simply the anticipation of future oil rents can shape behavior, constituting a kind of "presource" curse, by which the perceived future value of holding office increases, inducing incumbents to seek to monopolize office and latent challengers to step up their efforts (Cust and Mihalyi 2017).

Needless to say, different ways of conceptualizing oil have combined with data availability to shape a wide variety of measures, contributing to the heterogeneity of findings. There are three basic approaches to measures: as a ratio, treating oil as a share of some other quantity; as a dichotomous condition, treating countries as being oil producers or nonproducers; and as a continuous quantity, possibly normalized by population size.

Early statements of the rentier state emphasized oil income as a share of government income, reasoning that higher values of this ratio indicated states that relied less heavily on tax revenues and were thus more autonomous from their citizens. Treating oil rents as ratios was quite common in the first decade of quantitative research, with Ross (2001), Smith (2004), and Morrison (2009), for example, measuring oil export revenues as a share of GDP, while Jensen and Wantchekon (2004) and others measuring oil revenues as a share of exports.[2] All of these ratios confront problems of ambiguous and possibly erroneous interpretations, subject to endogeneity bias. Oil income as a share of exports would be heavily influenced by the size of the local economy and hence potentially its overall reliance on exports, and its level of development, in terms of income and level of industrialization, which would influence whether oil was consumed locally or exported. A similar problem plagues measurement of oil rents as a share of GDP, as poorer countries would appear more oil-rich because their lower incomes implied a smaller denominator and hence a larger ratio.

But perhaps most fundamentally, from a theoretical perspective, is that these ratio-based measures tell us little about how oil rents shape the incentives and capacities of rulers, rivals, and citizens. Rulers in two countries with identical oil export revenues and similar GDPs, but with very different population sizes, would have equally different rent capacities to employ for patronage or coercion

---

[2] Both ratio measures drew on publicly available data from the World Bank's Development Indicators, which, at the time, were the most comprehensive. On Smith's part, we can say that his measurement choice in 2004 was guided by an intent to use the same measure as Ross for reasons of comparability. Subsequently, Smith worked with the late Kevin Morrison in 2005 as he constructed the same measure, again for comparability.

(or modernization). Thus, this measure masked differences in the rentierism capacity of states.

Consequently, researchers have developed new and more suitable indicators that may align better with theoretical intuitions and avoid obvious sources of measurement error. Ross (2012, 15–17) recommends a measure of fuel income per capita, which takes the total value of oil and natural gas production (including domestic consumption) and divides it by a country's population to give a sense of the resources made available directly to rulers by the oil industry. Fuel income per capita, then, is a measure of abundance, not a measure of dependence. Yet as Smith (2017, 602) points out, this measure does not solve the problem that oil production is partially endogenous to political stability. Smith argues that for most of our theories, what is really at stake is the leverage that oil rents allow states to exercise over their citizens by affecting their material quotidian lives. Smith's new measure of rent leverage is calculated as the ratio of fuel income per capita to GDP per capita, corrected for purchasing power parity. This measure, which is prone to the same endogeneity problems as all ratio calculations, allows a direct answer to the critical question of what share of an average citizen's economic life derives directly from state-directed allocation of oil and gas income.

New measures continue to proliferate, however, and a recent one brings us back full circle to the idea of state fiscal reliance on oil rents. Lucas and Richter (2016) introduce the Global State Revenues and Expenditures data set, which they argue provides the most accurate measure of oil income directly controlled by governments by recording payments to the state above the sum of unit production costs and return to capital; this measure thus requires aggregating several different ways in which oil revenue can enter state budgets – as nontax revenues or as various types of tax revenues. To the extent that oil rents are kept off the budget to hide their true magnitude, this measure would provide the minimum amount of resources available to the state.

Dichotomous measures are not widely used and are generally treated with skepticism because they sacrifice too much relevant information, and some suffer from low construct validity. Fish (2002) uses OPEC membership despite the fact that more than half of oil producers then were not, and today more than three quarters are not members of OPEC. More generally, dichotomous measures such as whether oil exports are more than half of all exports create an arbitrary threshold, such that a ratio of 49.9 percent would be considered politically irrelevant while a ratio of 50.1 percent would be considered politically relevant.

Andersen and Ross (2014, 1002), however, claim that oil rents should be treated dichotomously (Ross 2012 suggests that $100 in per capita fuel income is the appropriate threshold), not continuously, because "when the fiscal powers of autocratically governed oil producers passed a *critical threshold* in the mid to late 1970s, they became capable of withstanding the democratic wave that swept the rest of the authoritarian world in the 1980s and 1990s" (p. 1002). While this dichotomous measure may suffer from the arbitrary exclusion of some countries just below the threshold, it reasonably posits that the existence of a nontrivial amount of fuel income per capita is the politically relevant condition; substantial rents versus trivial or no rents is more important than incremental increases in the level of rents, well above or well below this threshold. Thus, the potential for error at the threshold is the price one must pay for relaxing the assumption that the probability of autocratic survival is monotonically increasing over the magnitude of oil rents. Their analysis, however, relies on the use of a continuous measure, resulting in a misfit between causal logic and statistics.

Research Designs to Control for Endogeneity and Omitted Variable Bias

Studies of the resource curse draw inferences from observational data. Any statistical finding derived from associational data may reflect a true causal relationship plus bias, of unknown proportions. Bias can stem from three sources: (1) omitted variable bias, or the endogeneity of measures of oil wealth to other common causes of political regimes, including prior measures of political regimes; (2) measurement error; and (3) endogenous selection bias.

Given time-series, cross-sectional data, the most fundamental element of the research design is whether it will exploit within-unit variance across time, cross-case variance at a point in time, or both. To illustrate the centrality of this decision, consider the debate between Haber and Menaldo (2011) and Ross and Andersen (2014). Recall that the primary methodological critique Haber and Menaldo make of the existing literature is that it relies too heavily on short-term, cross-sectional comparison to study a longer-term, within-country effect. Much of their analysis consists of constructing country-specific time-series for oil-rich countries. In response, Andersen and Ross counter that Haber and Menaldo's inferences are all invalid because the proper comparison compares the propensity for democratic transitions among oil producers and nonproducers.

From the perspective of research design, however, Haber and Menaldo are not making any fundamental error by basing their estimates on longitudinal data that exploits within-country variance. Define a causal effect of treatment, t_i, a measure of oil wealth, on an outcome, y_i, a measure of political regime, as

$\delta_i = y_{it} - y_{ic}$, where the additional subscripts t and c refer to treatment and control. Because we cannot observe unit i under treatment and control simultaneously, one of the two observations must be missing; we have no direct information in the data about counterfactual outcomes. We are therefore compelled to select observations of other units at the same time or observations of the same unit at different times for the missing counterfactual – or, as a third option, a weighted average of both comparisons. Treating the estimates of a regression model as a causal effect thus requires a nonparametric identification strategy, or research design, that "allows the investigator to isolate a causal effect from an observed association without functional form assumptions" (Keele, Stevenson, and Elwert 2019, 3). Specifically, the research design is composed of a set of assumptions that, if satisfied, ensure that any potential causes of treatment are statistically independent of the values of Y, the potential outcomes. Identification strategies are arguments, not logical demonstrations: as such, they vary in how convincing they are. In general, designs are more convincing when they are premised on knowledge of the assignment mechanism and its independence from the potential outcomes, as exemplified by the procedure of random assignment to treatment.

It bears emphasizing that causal effects are defined on individual units: although scholars sometimes use the language of "cross-case effects," there is no such thing as a between-unit causal effect. Any difference between two units reflects either different treatment status or heterogeneous responses to treatment given covariates. This remains true as we move from static to dynamic analyses with lagged values of the dependent variable included as a regressor. In a time-series context, we define a causal effect for an individual country as the effects of a particular "treatment history," where $x_{1:t}$ is the history of oil wealth over time periods 1 through t, $x'_{1:t}$ is an alternative treatment history over the same set of time periods with a different value of treatment for at least one time period, and the time-dependent potential outcomes are defined as $Y_{it}(x_{1:t}) - Y_{it}(x'_{1:t})$: the difference between the outcome given an observed treatment history and the counterfactual outcome were that country to follow an alternative treatment history (Blackwell and Glynn 2018). An unbiased estimate of this causal effect would require satisfaction of sequential ignorability.

Whether we reach this estimate through a design that emphasizes within-case variance or cross-case variance is a function of the specific research design: there is no *a priori* warrant for dismissing within-case analysis (and, it should be said, Haber and Menaldo include panel analysis, including panels that cover the period beginning in 1973). Here we consider several such designs: selection on observables, selection on observables with fixed effects, instrumental variables, and selection on observables with synthetic control matching.

Selection on observables is the most basic strategy for the statistical analysis of observational data: identify a set of covariates such that treatment assignment is independent of the potential outcomes conditional on that set. By contemporary standards, the appropriate procedure would be to draw a causal graph, defend it theoretically, and then use graph theory to identify the subset of covariates that would be sufficient to achieve conditional independence in a model that controlled for them, using the criterion of d-separation (Keele, Stevenson, and Elwert 2019).

In general, the statistical models we have reviewed here do not satisfy the high standards for selection on observables. First, few scholars expend much effort to justify their selection of control variables as sufficient for conditional independence. Second, few scholars justify treating covariates as prior causes versus mediators or post-treatment effects, creating the strong possibility of post-treatment bias. Virtually all statistical models, for example, include national income as a covariate; the implied causal model is that income levels are a common cause of democracy and of oil wealth. Yet a moment's reflection might suggest that income is more appropriately viewed as an *effect* of oil wealth; a poor country that discovers oil can very quickly become a relatively wealthy country. Thus, controlling for income in a multivariate model introduces *post-treatment bias* (Paine 2016; Montgomery, Nyhan, and Torres 2018). Controlling for oil means that we compare oil-rich Saudi Arabia, for example, to rich nonproducers; yet the appropriate counterfactual to a Saudi Arabia without oil is a poor country – Yemen is the proper comparator, not Canada (Herb 2005). Post-treatment bias creates a misleading set of comparisons.

Third, all too often, scholars conflate two desiderata: causal identification, which requires only adjusting for common causes, and error correction, which requires including other potential causes of the outcome variable regardless of their relationship to the treatment variable. The latter strategy is sometimes preferred because it implies fewer omitted variables and hence more precise estimates with tighter confidence intervals and lower p-values. While lower p-values may generate a higher probability of being published, they provide little confidence that an estimate is unbiased in the absence of a well-defined research design.

Two conclusions follow. First, to the extent that different studies select different observables – or different measures of observables – we should expect heterogeneous findings because we are literally testing different causal models. Second, extreme caution should be exercised before accepting standard regression estimates as representing unbiased causal effects. It bears repeating that standard errors and derived confidence intervals and p-values are measures of our confidence that a reported estimate is statistically significant from 0, but they are not indicators of the unbiasedness of an estimate. Under the best of circumstances, selection on observables should be considered a weak and fragile design that produces systematically biased estimates.

Given panel data, scholars routinely estimate models with fixed effects. These designs exploit the fact that any variable, observed or unobserved, that does not change its value over time will have a mean equal to the invariant value. By simply subtracting observed values from the mean to extract within-case variance, these differenced variables all take on the value of 0: fixed-effects models, therefore, easily control for all time-invariant sources of potential bias, and they imply an unambiguous interpretation as within-unit changes over time.

Beyond this mathematical and conceptual simplicity, however, there are many questions about these designs. First, we note that there are heterogeneous findings even among fixed-effects models, with some models supporting the resource curse and others finding no evidence for it: on their own, fixed-effects models do not solve any of our problems.[3] Second, fixed-effects models become statistically more complex in dynamic models that include lagged values of the dependent variable because the error term will be correlated with the lagged dependent variable. In response, econometricians have developed a class of generalized methods-of-moments estimators; naturally, there is debate about which generalized GMM estimator to use, with Haber and Menaldo (2011) using the Arellano–Bond estimator and Aslaksen (2010) reaching contradictory conclusions using the supposedly superior Blundell and Bond estimator. Here, we note that these GMM estimators are highly complex "black-box" estimators, easy to implement in Stata or R, but also easy to misuse and very hard to interpret (Roodman 2009). Scholars actively involved in developing these estimators caution that in applied research, these estimators may "provide misleading information on the actual precision of the often seriously biased estimators" (Kiviet, Pleus, and Poldermans 2017, 2).

Finally, if we believe that our fixed-effects models have controlled for time-invariant sources of bias, there are still inferential hurdles to overcome. Most obviously, we must still properly control for time-variant sources of bias. Furthermore, when fixed-effects models are used in a dynamic framework, additional assumptions must be satisfied: that past treatments do not directly influence current outcomes, and that past outcomes do not affect current treatment (Imai and Kim 2019). Without reason to believe these assumptions have been satisfied, fixed-effects regression models are not sources of unbiased causal inference.

---

[3] Ross (2012) primarily estimates models without fixed effects and finds support for the resource curse; when he adds fixed effects, the estimates are not statistically significant.

A third design searches for exogenous sources of oil wealth using instrumental variables. An instrument for a potentially endogenous variable like oil wealth is a third variable that satisfies two conditions: it is related to the potentially endogenous measure of oil (the inclusion or relevance condition), and it is not related to the measure of democracy or to the error in the main regression equation other than by way of its effect on oil (the exclusion condition). If both conditions are met, the predicted values from a regression of the endogenous variable on the instrument will be an exogenous source of variation. The first condition is easily checked directly; the second condition presents more of a challenge because to establish that the instrument is statistically independent of the error term, we would have to know all the omitted variables that contribute to the error term. Therefore, the most convincing instrumental-variable designs make highly plausible *arguments* about why the instrument cannot be correlated with the outcome variable. It is the transparency and the plausibility of the argument that makes the design convincing, and arguments about exogenous instruments based solely on black-box statistical techniques (by using lagged values of the variables and lagged values of the differenced equations) should be treated with a higher degree of skepticism.

Consider measures of oil reserves, discoveries, or endowments. To be sure, levels of reserves or peak discoveries of oil are, to some extent, governed by geological factors. But the rate of exploration and information about reserves are both likely to be endogenous and thus will not satisfy the exclusion restriction. Brooks and Kurtz (2016) argue convincingly that oil endowments are not exogenous gifts of nature but rather may be endogenous to the technology used to detect and extract them; more indirectly, endowments may be endogenous to the level of human capital formation and state policies. Liou and Musgrave (2014, online appendix pages 137–141) provide considerable evidence that *measurement* of reserves is the key variable, and these depend on existing prices and hence the commercial viability of new exploration and extraction. As they show, proven reserves can rise or fall in response to changed market, technological, or political conditions without any new discovery or extraction taking place. This is all true whether we use proven oil reserves or measures of total oil endowments, which are complex extrapolations from proven reserves (Tsui 2011). Finally, Smith (2017) observes that the decision to explore for new reserves requires an assessment of the risk of future political instability, and hence may be endogenous to current politics.

Kristopher Ramsay (2011) models exogenous price hikes caused by out-of-region natural disasters that disrupt oil production; the out-of-region condition is imposed to satisfy the exclusion restriction. But as Haber and Menaldo (2011) point out, temporary supply disruptions will likely trigger countervailing responses by the largest oil producers, especially Saudi Arabia which has long had a policy of adjusting its production to elicit stability in world oil markets; Ramsay's models, therefore, may be rendered invalid by a "big Middle East producer" fixed effect. For example, even a rocket attack on Saudi Arabia's own production facilities – which took half its production offline in September 2019 – was resolved within days and the immediate price spike lasted less than a week. Furthermore, while Ramsay models short-term price fluctuations, Wacziarg (2012) argues that long-term price series are set by global markets and are therefore exogenous; models based on this design fail to demonstrate a resource curse. Testing the relationship between Polity scores and an annual index of crude oil prices, he finds no long-term relationship: price hikes do not appear to be systematically and inversely related to Polity scores.

We think that newly published data on sedimentary basins provides a potentially valid instrument. Basins, however, are a vector of characteristics and devising an instrument requires statistical theory to select the optimal set and avoid the problem of weak instruments. Cassidy (2019, 2756), for example, maximizes the F statistic with an instrument set consisting of "the singleton basin type with convergent continent-continent tectonics and mechanical subsidence." Furthermore, identification requires the addition of controls because the distribution of sedimentary basins around the world is highly uneven and hence basins may be correlated with other possible determinants of democracy – fertile agricultural plains conducive to both complex societies and states and also to long-range prosperity, for example. Finally, because basin size is a constant, this instrument can only be used with a simple cross-sectional design. Using a normalized Polity scale, Cassidy measures democracy twice, in 1966 and in 2008, while the model includes predicted values of the logged value of average oil production per capita, 1966–2008. The result of this cross-sectional design is that an increase in oil production by one standard deviation would be associated with a reduced Polity score of about 0.16, or one-half of a standard deviation.

We are most persuaded by Liao and Musgrave's use of the synthetic control method, in part because their use of the method is entirely transparent and well-justified. Liao and Musgrave use the 1973 oil embargo and massive price hike as an exogenous event that constitutes "treatment" for a select set of countries. The relevant countries are those that were "latent" producers prior to 1973, becoming significant producers only after the event. To establish the exogeneity of the event, Liao and Musgrave use standard time-series techniques to test for a structural break in the time series; *pace* Andersen and Ross, the structural break in the time-series data occurred in 1973, not 1979 or 1980. Furthermore, the balance of qualitative evidence they present clearly supports the claim that the price shock was *exogenous* to all oil producers outside of the Arab Gulf oil producers, in that marginal producers could neither affect the timing of the shock nor increase pre-shock production in anticipation of a massive price increase about which they were unaware.

In order for a country to be "treated" by the price shock, it must have a latent oil industry and it must not have been fiscally reliant on oil rents at a high level prior to the price shock: countries without oil endowments are "never treats" that cannot be affected by an exogenous price shock, while countries that were rentier states before the price shock are "always treats." Neither type of case is relevant. Seven countries comprise the category of "compliers" – countries that would become significant oil producers only after a price shock: Algeria, Ecuador, Gabon, Indonesia, Mexico, Nigeria, and Trinidad. The donor pool contains forty-four countries that would be informative controls: most importantly, they must not be resource-dependent, and they must not have been long-term consolidated democracies. For each of the seven treated countries, a composite control that minimizes the mean square predicted error for the pre-shock period was generated: the synthetic control matches, to the greatest extent possible, observed Polity scores for the years prior to the price shock. Given simple time-series plots, we can then easily observe whether the treated countries diverge from their synthetic control in the years following the shock and then subject observed differences to placebo tests for statistical significance, which can also be depicted in time-series plots (Abadie, Diamond, and Hainmueller 2015). This carefully constructed design provides virtually no evidence of a resource curse.

Measurement and Endogenous Selection Bias

In addition to designs that potentially correct for endogeneity or omitted variable bias, studies claiming a causal effect of oil must deal with the potential for bias stemming from measurement error or endogenous selection. Consider first measurement error, specifically the problem of missing data. Missing data is related to measurement error in one of two ways: either we can construe measurement error as a type of missing data problem where observed values provide probabilistic information about missing values, or we can think of missing data as an extreme form of measurement error for which we have no proxy information from mismeasured observations (Blackwell, Honaker, and King 2017).

Ranjit Lall (2017) has carefully considered the consequences of missing data for analyses of the political resource curse. Surveying several prominent analyses, he finds a high degree of missing data that is not randomly distributed:

overall, autocracies are far more likely to have missing data than democracies. Furthermore, dealing with nonrandom missing data through listwise deletion results in both loss of statistical efficiency and bias; specifically, these data sets have a type of selection bias – a pro-democracy bias – because after listwise deletion, democracies are over-represented. Lall corrects this selection problem through multiple imputation and reanalyzes several prominent articles. In general, Lall concludes that his reanalysis by affirming that oil has two anti-democratic effects – weakening democracies and strengthening autocracies – and these effects are more prominent after 1980. We consider this an important correction to the literature, and we urge more authors to consider superior methods for handling missing data. However, we think it imperative that efforts to correct the problem of missing data be performed in conjunction with other efforts to construct research designs that correct for omitted variable bias.

Consider next endogenous selection bias. Standard methodological advice in political science is to avoid selecting on the dependent variable, which is usually a problem when scholars intentionally select a small number of case studies. Yet the broader phenomenon of endogenous selection can occur in statistical studies that appear to include "all cases." The problem is caused by conditioning on a variable that, in a given causal system, is a collider (because two or more arrows enter it), or on a descendant of a collider (on collider bias, see Pearl 2000, 17; Elwert and Winship 2014; Pearl and Mackenzie 2018, 185–86, 197–200).

Consider Figure 1, below, which represents the politics of the Arabian Gulf in the interwar period. It contains a box around the node "Survival" because we implicitly condition on survival in all Comparative Politics data sets: to be included in a data set, a country must have survived as a sovereign country into the contemporary period. Differential rates of survival can induce a form of selection bias, usually called "survivorship bias" (King, Keohane, and Verba 1994). To see why, note that survival is a descendant of the node Protection, and that Protection is a collider variable: arrows enter in from Oil and from British Policy. The model represents a version of the null hypothesis: it represents the claim that oil is not causally related to autocratic resilience (represented by the absence of an arrow), either directly or indirectly.[4] Yet by conditioning on the descendant of a collider, we induce statistical association between oil and autocratic resilience by opening the path Oil -> Protection -> British Policy -> Autocratic Resilience. Without conditioning on the collider variable, Oil and British Policy are statistically independent of one another, as indicated by the lack of an arrow between them. If this model is correctly specified, therefore, the

---

[4] Note that we use the term "autocratic resilience" in place of "autocratic survival" to avoid confusion between the two ways that "survival" is used here: survival to become a sovereign country and survival of a particular autocratic regime spell.

Figure 1 Endogenous sovereignty

observed statistical association between oil and autocratic resilience represents bias (false positives), not a causal relationship.

We believe that the historical evidence supports the causal model in Figure 1 as an accurate description of the twentieth-century political history of Kuwait, Bahrain, Qatar, the United Arab Emirates, and Oman. All too briefly, the evidence we present elsewhere clearly confirms that in the early age of oil, British policy toward the five principalities of the eastern seaboard underwent a large shift toward preserving their independence and intervening in domestic affairs to elicit political stability; that British protection was absolutely crucial to maintaining the independence of the five principalities against Saudi aggression; and that British intervention in domestic politics established the institutional framework for long-term monarchical stability. We think as well that these are the only instances of survivorship bias in the developing world; our search for other cases has not turned up any plausible candidates (for details on the causal model and the supporting historical evidence, see Waldner and Smith 2020). We provide the statistical evidence of survivorship bias and the false positives it induces in Section 5: for now, we conclude with the point that the bias induced by endogenous selection is as injurious to causal inference as the bias induced by omitted common causes. Even if we accepted that existing research designs have adequately controlled for omitted variables, we would still have to deal with the possibility of selection bias.

Conclusion

In this section, we have reviewed three major ingredients of the study of the political resource curse: theories of the resource curse, conceptualization and measurement of the main variables, and research designs. The most straightforward conclusion we can draw is that the heterogeneity of inputs in large part accounts for the heterogeneity of findings. In some sense, researchers have too many degrees of freedom; mixing and matching these different elements into distinct and plausible models yields equally diverse results. Given that scholars start from diverse theoretical positions; and given that these theoretical positions have implications for observable implications and thus how scholars construct models to test their hypotheses; and given that these models can incorporate diverse conceptualizations and measures of oil wealth and of democracy; and given that that scholars propose a variety of research designs: given all of this variation in inputs, it is simply not surprising to find heterogeneous findings, many of which support the political resource curse, some of which appear to contradict it, and others which find a conditional relationship in which oil may have a negative effect, a positive effect, or a null effect, depending on a case's location in the relevant parameter space. Indeed, we wish to emphasize that even if we focus only on findings that support the political resource curse, we will still find a great deal of heterogeneity. Not all of the findings are in fact identical to one another or necessarily consistent with one another.

Beyond this simple and uncontroversial conclusion, we have made some suggestions about theories, measures, and designs. They are not all equally good; some measures create problems, some designs do not resolve problems, etc. We have deliberately avoided stark pronouncements: our goal is to clarify the issues and to encourage greater deliberation by the research community itself. We should all be actively involved in specifying better theories, better measures, and better designs.

4 Refinement

This section pivots from surveying the existing literature and critically evaluating its component parts to presenting some elements of a new agenda for studying the relationship of oil and politics. We make three basic points. First, we argue that existing studies of the resource curse have under-estimated the degree of causal heterogeneity. To understand the potential causal effect of oil wealth, we will have to grapple more satisfactorily with temporal and spatial heterogeneity. Second, we argue that existing theoretical frameworks used to explain the resource curse are unsatisfactory in large part because they are inconsistent with causal heterogeneity. To understand the potential causal effect of oil wealth, we will have to move beyond the existing theoretical enclave to incorporate context-specific theories of political coalitions and institutions. Third, to develop and test more complex theories that are sensitive to temporal and regional heterogeneity requires, we argue, shifting from an exclusive reliance on multivariate regression models to multi-method studies that incorporate qualitative evidence and inference.

Scope Conditions? Tracking the Resource Curse across Time and Space

We have reason to believe that the political resource curse varies, perhaps substantially so, across time and space; there is no single relationship between oil and politics. Consider the United States: in a twenty-five-year span beginning in 1890, the United States overtook Great Britain and became the most productive economy in the world. At the same time, the United States was the world's dominant producer of industrial minerals, including oil (Wright and Czelusta 2007). The onset of the American oil industry literally fueled economic growth without disturbing the country's democratic development, itself only recently fractured by the Civil War.

As we have seen, Andersen and Ross (2014; see also Ross 2012) claim that the American experience is not anomalous because a structural break in the oil–democracy linkage occurred in approximately 1980: the political resource curse, they propose, is entirely a post-1980 phenomenon. Three pieces of evidence subtend this claim. First, simple bivariate statistics show that the Polity scores of oil producers and nonproducers begin to diverge significantly only in the early 1980s. Second, Andersen and Ross estimate time-series models that show a structural break in approximately 1981. Finally, they provide a brief, two-stage history of international oil markets: an earlier period in which a handful of oligopolistic oil conglomerates captured most of the rents of oil production and a later period in which the balance of power shifted substantially in favor of oil producers, culminating in a wave of nationalizations, the creation of national oil companies, and the oil price hikes of the 1970s.

This is a powerful web of evidence, but it must be weighed carefully against contrary evidence. First, in their statistical tests, Andersen and Ross do not examine a basic long-term time-series of commodity prices with structural break tests; when Liou and Musgrave (2014) use several such tests, they find a structural break in oil prices in 1974, not 1980. Second, we find a significant number of claims that a resource curse exists prior to 1980. Mahdavy's pioneering article on the Iranian rentier state was published in 1970 and drew on data going back several decades. Anderson's (1987) work on Libya, Crystal's (1990) work on Kuwait and Qatar, and Karl's (1997) work on Venezuela all present evidence of oil's effects on politics in the pre–World War II period. Goldberg, Wibbels, and Mvukiyehe (2008) find evidence of a resource curse supporting incumbents as early as 1928 in oil-producing American states. Wigley (2018) finds a negative relationship of oil to multiple measures of individual rights and liberties in a panel analysis stretching back to 1932.

Third, while there is no doubt that the structure of international oil markets had undergone significant change by 1980, there are still reasons to doubt that these changes imply the absence of a resource curse prior to 1980. Much depends on precisely how we define what changed over the three or more decades preceding 1980. Andersen and Ross (2014, 1001) claim that prior to

1980, international oil companies used their hegemonic position to "capture most of the rents for themselves," while after the structural changes, including the nationalization of oil endowments and the construction of national oil companies, "the size of government revenues grew dramatically." Thus, Andersen and Ross contrast two conceptually distinct measures: the pre-1980 division of resource rents between states and oil companies and the post-1980 growth of the absolute magnitude of oil rents and the relative share of oil rents in government revenues and expenditures. This comparison is problematic because pre-1980 oil producers might have received a small *relative* share of oil rents that were still, in *absolute* terms, large enough to induce a political resource curse.

Early concession agreements were ridiculously small: Socal received a concession for Saudi oil worth as much as $1 trillion in exchange for under $1 million, while the Kuwaiti emir handed over control of its oil endowment to Gulf Oil and Anglo-Persian for an advance of $180,000 and annual payments of $100,000. Yet we have good evidence that while these sums were a tiny share of overall resource wealth, in absolute terms, they were sufficient to entrench ruling dynasties in power (Krane 2019, 37). Furthermore, by 1938, with the nationalization of the Mexican oil industry, these initial bargains became obsolete at an accelerating rate. Five years later, Venezuela negotiated a new arrangement with Standard Oil and Shell granting it 50 percent of revenues (though undoubtedly the oil companies still understated those revenues subject to even sharing), Saudi Arabia, Kuwait, and Iraq achieved this 50 percent threshold by 1952, and other producers followed suit. Mahdavy (1970, 431) observed in his pioneering article that the period 1950–6, during which Iran initially nationalized its oil industry and Egypt nationalized the Suez Canal Company, constitutes the key turning point in the history of the rentier state in the Middle East, such that "the current payments of the oil companies in the first five years after 1956 were *over seven times as much as the payments during the entire thirty-six years before 1950.*" While the 50–50 deal persisted into the early 1970s, by 1969, Libya had succeeded in forcing an increase in the posted price of oil in an effort to subvert multinational efforts to hide their true income (Krane 2019, 40–42).

Thus, even prior to the 1973 price shock, and certainly by the mid-1950s, governments of oil producers had access to significant amounts of oil income. True, these would pale in significance to post-1973 revenues, but this is not the relevant question: the relevant question is whether pre-1973 or even pre-1980 oil income would have been sufficient to provoke a visible resource curse if such a causal effect exists. Unfortunately, we do not know the threshold above which oil rents are sufficient to induce an observable political resource curse.

Therefore, we do not think the evidence unambiguously supports the claim that the resource curse is exclusively a post-1980 phenomenon: if the political resource curse exists, it should have been observable prior to 1980, and works that study the pre-1980 period without observing a resource curse cannot be rejected on these grounds.

An alternative possibility that also implies temporal heterogeneity is that the oil rents have an effect that is relatively constant across time, but a second process exerts more powerful countervailing causal influence in some time periods but not others: therefore, the political resource curse will be unobservable when the second effect is present and observable when it is absent. Cullen Hendrix (2018) argues that during the Cold War, the system-level rivalry between the US and the USSR led to support for all dictatorships, resource-rich and resource poor. The termination of the Cold War in 1990 ended support for dictatorships; while many resource-poor regime dictatorships then succumbed to pressure to democratize, oil-rich dictatorships resisted any democratizing pressures. Therefore, we should observe either no political resource curse or only a very weak effect prior to 1990; an observable effect would largely be a phenomenon of the past three decades.

The second dimension of potential causal heterogeneity is spatial: for our purposes, this is the possibility that the resource curse varies by region. In a meta-analysis of twenty-nine studies of the political resource curse, Anar Ahmadov (2014) found powerful evidence for regional differences, with dummy variables for Latin America, sub-Saharan Africa, and the Middle East and North Africa (MENA) showing significant impacts on partial correlations, while East and South Asia along with Eastern Europe and the former Soviet Union do not change the results. Benjamin Smith (2012) has also noted a similar effect for Southeast Asia. As we will show, taking 1980 as the onset of the Third Wave of democratization in the post-colonial world, we see distinct regional patterns across these four global regions.[5]

Figure 2 depicts the Polity scores of seven Latin American oil producers since 1960. We have already discussed Venezuela's "precocious" democratic transition; what is striking about Figure 2 is that Latin America's other oil producers also experienced a democratic transition, most of them soon after 1980. The notable exception is Trinidad and Tobago, which has been stably democratic since independence in 1960. Michael Ross has already drawn our attention to this "Latin American exceptionalism," noting that not only have all Latin American oil producers become democracies, but, since 1980, they were three

---

[5] We omit some oil producers, such as Ghana and Chad, from our presentation here because they became significant oil producers only well after the Third Wave.

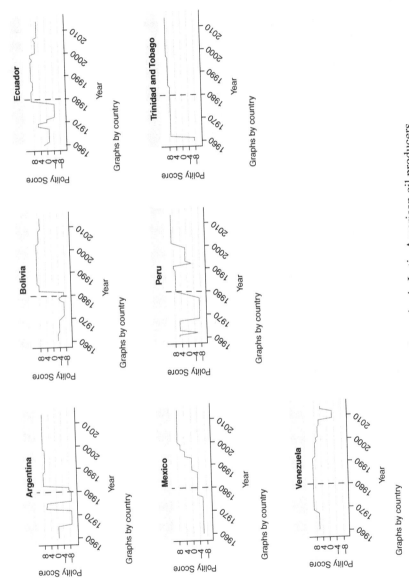

Figure 2 Regime dynamics in Latin American oil producers

times more likely to experience a democratic transition than nonproducers in Latin America.

In stark contrast to Latin American exceptionalism, the vast majority of oil producers in the MENA region have remained stubbornly autocratic. Consider first the six oil producers of the Arabian Peninsula: Kuwait, Bahrain, Qatar, the United Arab Emirates, Oman, and Saudi Arabia. These six countries exemplify the political resource curse to an astounding degree. Kuwait, Saudi Arabia, and the UAE alone accounted for about 40 percent of total oil reserves in 2005 (Smil 2008, 114). These six members of the Gulf Cooperation Council (GCC-6) are also among the world's most intractable autocracies, as illustrated in Figure 3. The three graphs in the top panel depict a highly constrained amount of variance, with just a handful of annual scores higher than –8. The three countries in the bottom panel are literally flat lines at extremely low scores: from the point of view of democracy, these countries have expired. Furthermore, leadership succession in these monarchies, has been, in almost every instance, orderly, with rulers departing due to ill health or advanced age and all replacements coming from close family members.

Outside of the GCC-6, the MENA region contains additional evidence for the resource curse, as illustrated in Figure 4. None of the six oil producers depicted in Figure 4 has received a Polity score that reaches the +8 threshold to be classified as a democracy. Iraq has slowly crept up the democracy scale, but only 15 years after the American-led overthrow of the Ba'thist dictatorship and the onset of American nation-building. Algeria and Iran have spent some time in positive territory, but still well below the threshold for democracy. After its brief experiment in multiparty parliamentary politics, Egypt has reverted to autocratic status, while Libya and Syria have suffered massive internal conflicts in the wake of their brief authoritarian openings. Within this overall picture of unrelieved autocracy, Tunisia stands apart following its democratic transition in 2014, as illustrated in Figure 5. While social scientists often omit Tunisia from the global community of significant oil producers, even as late as 2009, well after its 1970s–80s oil heyday, its per capita oil income was on par with such oil states as Indonesia, Sudan, and Brazil (Ross 2012, 20–22).

Outcomes among oil producers in Africa fall between the two extremes of Latin American exceptionalism and the exemplary rentier states of the Middle East. Figure 6 illustrates how Africa's major oil producers fared as the region's autocracies encountered the Third Wave after the fall of the Berlin Wall in late 1989. These graphs are quite distinct from the Middle Eastern graphs: in every instance, we observe a nontrivial increase in democracy scores surrounding 1990, the year when the end of the Cold War triggered large-scale protest movements, political reforms, and transitions to multiparty politics (Bratton

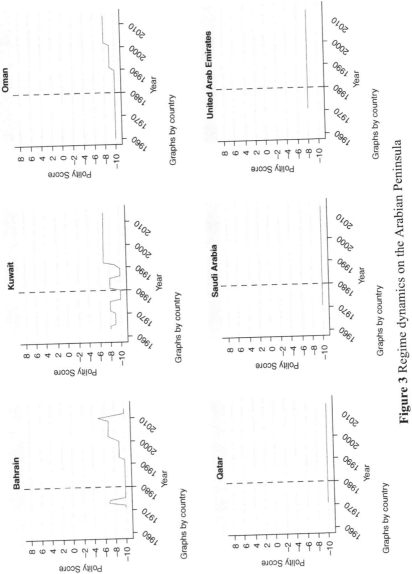

Figure 3 Regime dynamics on the Arabian Peninsula

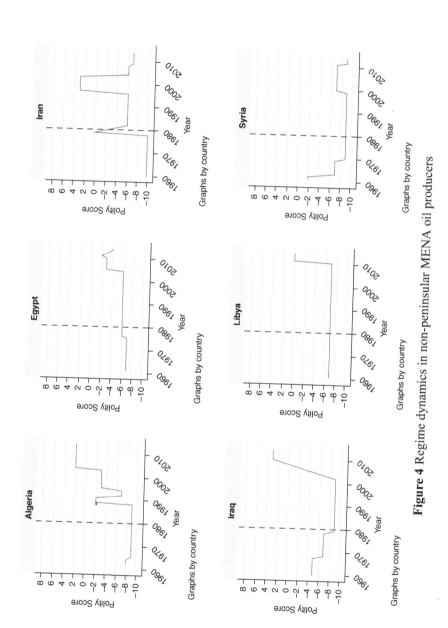

Figure 4 Regime dynamics in non-peninsular MENA oil producers

Politics of Development

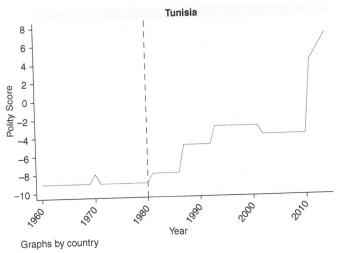

Graphs by country

Figure 5 Regime dynamics in Tunisia

and van de Walle 1997). On the other hand, in contrast to Latin America, only Nigeria experienced a sustained improvement that approached the +8 threshold for democracy, with the other five countries either hitting a plateau that falls short of the threshold for a democratic transition or suffering autocratic regression, albeit never fully returning to their pre-1990 levels. In contrast to Latin American exceptionalism and the exemplary rentier states of the MENA region, African oil producers have had an erratic experience with democracy.

Finally, examining five Southeast Asian cases in Figure 7, we find another variety of outcomes. Polity does not include Brunei in its country coverage, but we have normalized its Freedom House data to the Polity scale for inclusion here. On one side are cases of relative stability, with little change between pre- and post-1980 scores in Malaysia, Papua New Guinea (both with relatively stable scores in the near vicinity of the democratic threshold), and Brunei. On the other side are cases of sharp discontinuities and transitions in Indonesia and Thailand, with democratic gains consolidated in the first but Thailand experiencing multiple swings between civilian democratic and military autocratic rule.

The evidence we have just adduced strongly suggests considerable regional variation in the political resource curse: regions differ in terms of the general tendency toward democratic transition during the Third Wave and in terms of the difference oil wealth appears to make during those transitions. Viewed from this regional perspective, the general claim about a resource curse becomes a set of interlocking puzzles in which oil perhaps interacts with a constellation of antecedent conditions. Solving these puzzles is one way to deepen our

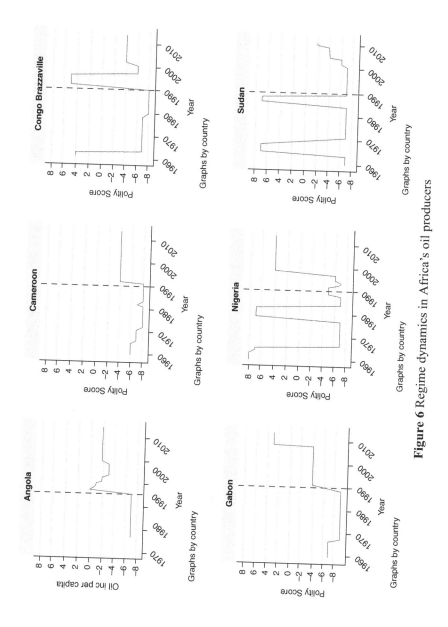

Figure 6 Regime dynamics in Africa's oil producers

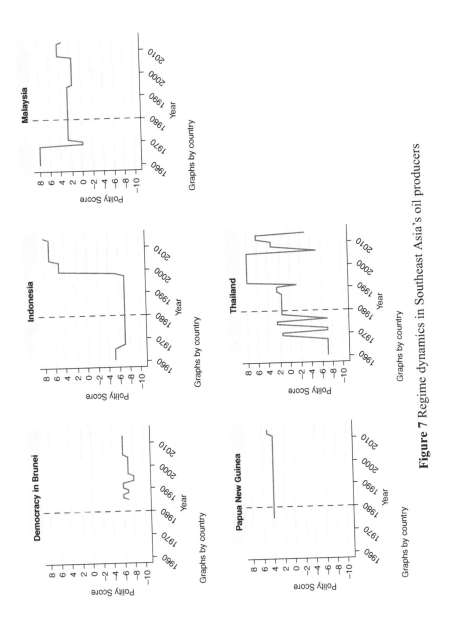

Figure 7 Regime dynamics in Southeast Asia's oil producers

understanding of the resource curse; their solution would seem to require our taking context much more deeply into consideration.

Revisiting Theories of Democracy in Light of Causal Heterogeneity

In Section 3 we discussed four versions of the theory of the political resource curse: (anti-) modernization theory, redistributive conflict theory, a fiscal theory of democracy, and intra-elite conflict theories of autocratic survival and breakdown. In this section, we revisit each theory and consider its relevance and utility in light of the causal heterogeneity we have just discussed.

Broadly speaking, modernization theory proposes that higher incomes are associated with democracy. As Adam Przeworski and Fernando Limongi (1997) first pointed out, this association can occur for two distinct reasons: rising incomes can directly cause autocracies to fail and to be replaced by democracies (endogenous modernization theory) or rising incomes can be statistically independent from democratic transitions, but once democracies are established for other reasons, rising income lowers the probability of democratic breakdowns (exogenous modernization theory). Studying the period 1950–90, Przeworski and Limongi found support for exogenous modernization theory but not for endogenous modernization theory: rising incomes stabilize democracies without causing democratic transitions. Carles Boix and Susan Stokes (2003; see also Boix 2011) modified these conclusions, confirming claims about exogenous modernization theory (wealthier democracies were less likely to break down), but arguing for a period-specific endogenous modernization theory: rising incomes had a strong relationship to democratic transitions prior to World War I, a moderate relationship in the interwar period, and a negligible relationship after 1950; to the contrary, the Third Wave of democracy first emerged during decades of global economic recession among countries undergoing substantial economic contraction (Haggard and Kaufmann 1995). Consequently, more recent democratic transitions have taken place at comparatively lower levels of national income (Bermeo and Yashar 2016).

These facts are inconvenient for an anti-modernization theory of the resource curse. As we have seen, scholarship on the resource curse has not always distinguished between two possible effects, inversely analogous to endogenous and exogenous modernization theory: in one effect, oil wealth causes democracies to become dictatorships, counteracting an exogenous modernization theory, and in the other effect, oil wealth helps autocrats remain in power, counteracting endogenous modernization theory. While exogenous modernization theory is broadly supported, we have substantial evidence that oil wealth does not cause democracies to become dictatorships.

And while we have many studies claiming that oil wealth helps autocrats remain in power, if endogenous modernization theory does not predict that in the period of main concern to the resource curse, rising incomes are making democratic transitions more likely, then there is no democratizing tendency for oil wealth to counteract.

In short, deriving a theory of the resource curse from modernization theory runs into a host of insoluble problems; and even if these problems were somehow solved in the future, a theoretical apparatus derived from modernization theory would not necessarily provide any analytic leverage over the issue of regional heterogeneity.

Much the same can be said about redistributive conflict. Here too we find the need to distinguish whether economic inequality is related to democratic transitions, to democratic consolidation, or to both. We also find substantial evidence of period-specific effects. Most importantly, there is good reason to believe that arguments about income inequality and redistributive conflict are not relevant to the post-colonial context in general or to the Third Wave of democracy in particular, where neither democratic breakdowns nor democratic transitions appear to be related to economic inequality and the redistributive conflicts they allegedly induce (Slater, Smith, and Nair 2014; Haggard and Kaufman 2012). It is somewhat hard to accept that outcomes of the resource curse depend upon the interaction of oil and inequality if, in general, inequality and redistributive conflict do not appear relevant to democratic transitions over the past few decades. If this is true in general, then inequality and redistributive conflict appear poor candidates to explain regional heterogeneity.

Perhaps the most familiar theoretical claim of the resource curse is that linking taxation to representation, or what we have called the Fiscal Theory of Democracy. The claim is rooted primarily in studies of early modern Europe, as exemplified by Charles Tilly (1990, 68) who posited that a relatively weak English state offered representative institutions to induce cooperation from capital-holders in financing war; the more general "bargaining model of representation" depicts rulers as compelled to exchange representation for access to resources controlled by societal actors (Boucoyannis 2015). As we have seen, Ross (2012) modifies this bargaining model to explain why incumbent autocrats with access to oil rents can satisfy citizens' preferences for spending without taxation and hence without democracy.

Its widespread popularity notwithstanding, there are crucial theoretical and empirical problems with the bargaining model and the derived fiscal theory of democracy. Studies of the relationship between war, state-building, and democracy in Western Europe suffer from unequal survivorship bias; most medieval and early-modern European polities did not become modern sovereign nation states, and of those that did, most followed historical trajectories that did not include the exchange of representative institutions for resources to finance war. Early-modern representative institutions, moreover, were tightly restricted to elites and there was no linear path to late nineteenth and early twentieth-century modern mass democracies: the bargaining model, if correctly specified, would have limited applicability. Yet Boucoyannis argues persuasively that the bargaining model mis-specifies the emergence of representative institutions in early modern Europe: the evidence she adduces clearly demonstrates that powerful rulers initially *compelled* landed magnates to attend assemblies and approve taxes; magnates denied rulers at great peril, because they occupied what was legally royal land and their occupancy could be contested.

Accordingly, if the fiscal theory of democracy were true, we should expect to observe an association between modern political regimes and levels of taxation; but the relevant research has reached ambiguous conclusions. Rival theories interpret the relationship of regime to revenue differently, with neoclassical accounts extending the bargaining model into the contemporary era of mass democracy and redistributive conflict accounts anticipating that under democracy, poor citizens impose redistributive taxation on the rich.

Empirically, results are scattered as well. Some studies find no observable difference in resource extraction between democracies and dictatorships (Cheibub 1998) and no evidence that greater tax burdens are causally related to higher levels of democracy (Ross 2004), and others finding some evidence that regressive consumption taxes are increased in the decade *following* democratic transitions (Timmons 2010).

Therefore, we have neither theory nor evidence supporting the claim that higher levels of taxation are a causal precursor to democratization. Indeed, as Boucoyannis observes, the American claim of "no taxation without representation" was followed by revolution, not by bargaining and the extension of British representative institutions to the colonies; American representative practices grew out of preexisting colonial institutions, not bargaining with revenue-hungry rulers. Given these problems with the general theory, it seems highly unlikely that the fiscal theory of democracy will be relevant to explaining regional heterogeneity.

The theory of the political resource curse thus confronts two distinct challenges. First, even while acknowledging the large body of research that finds evidence for a political resource curse, we have pointed to a number of areas – contradictory and inconsistent findings, methodologically flawed analyses, and the absence of a credible theoretical framework – that continue to cast doubt on the core claims of the resource curse. Second, even if we were to concede that a resource curse exists, we would still have to deal with the issue of regional –

and perhaps temporal – heterogeneity: oil does not appear to have the same observable implications across time and space. In the remainder of this section, we deal with the problem of theoretical indeterminism and causal heterogeneity; in Section 5, we take a fresh look at whether a resource curse exists as a general phenomenon.

The Next Theoretical Frontier? Political Institutions and Coalitions

We have discussed support for two claims: first, autocratic oil producers experience regime failure at a lower rate than nonproducers, and second, among autocratic oil producers, there are distinctive regional patterns in political reforms and democratic transitions, ranging from Latin American exceptionalism to the exemplary rentier states of the MENA region, with erratic transitions in Africa and dichotomized outcomes in Southeast Asia falling between these two extremes. We think that the most promising theoretical approach to these variations is the literature on autocratic regime durability. That literature is too large and too diverse to cover here completely, but we can quickly gain analytic leverage by taking into account two types of variables: political institutions and political coalitions.

Perhaps the core claim of the literature on autocratic regime durability is that different subtypes of autocratic regimes exhibit different dynamics of intra-elite competition and hence have different propensities for survival. Barbara Geddes (1999), for example, distinguished military regimes, personalist regimes, and single-party regimes, as well as amalgams of these three subtypes. In her empirical analysis using a dataset that distinguished intra-autocratic transitions from democratic transitions, Geddes found that military regimes were, on average, the least durable, single-party regimes the most durable, and personalist regimes occupying an intermediary position. Subsequent work with Erika Frantz and Joseph Wright (Wright, Frantz, and Geddes 2015) has elaborated this basic typology (in part by describing the special durability of monarchies) and has considered the independent role of oil wealth.

Let us assume that oil wealth extends the lifespan of all autocratic types by allowing rulers to purchase the loyalty of regime insiders and societal groups and also to purchase the means of repression; but let us also assume that oil wealth does not change the order of subtype specific durability: among oil producers, we would expect military regimes to have the shortest duration and single-party regimes and monarchies to have the longest duration.

Evidence from our four regions is fully consistent with this thesis. The vast majority of autocratic regimes in Latin America on their eve of the most recent transitions to democracy, both oil producers and nonproducers, were military regimes and hence would have the shortest expected lifespan. A minority of countries had single-party regimes, and as expected, these tended to produce highly durable autocracies, including Cuba, which remains autocratic, and Mexico, which alone among the oil producers delayed its democratic transition until 2000. In stark contrast, autocratic regimes in the Middle East tend to be monarchies or single-party regimes, the two subtypes with the highest likelihood of autocratic survival. All members of the GCC-6 are a specific form of monarchy, what Michael Herb (1999) calls "dynastic monarchies" – monarchies on steroids – in that members of the royal family staff key ministerial, bureaucratic, and military positions. Outside the Arabian Peninsula, Middle Eastern oil-producing autocracies have all been some version of a single-party regime: the FLN in Algeria, the Neo-Destour in Tunisia, the National Democratic Party in Egypt, and the Ba'th Party in Iraq and Syria. Only Algeria after 1992 is coded as a military regime.

African autocracies follow no simple pattern: of the six oil producers in Figure 6, three were personalist or military regimes in 1989, while the other three were single-party regimes. Yet underneath this mélange of autocratic institutions, Michael Bratton and Nicolas van de Walle (1997) posit that virtually all African dictatorships were neopatrimonial regimes in which authority is vested not in an office or a set of rules but in the person of the chief executive, who exercises rule through patronage, not through ideology or formal political and administrative institutions. In the wake of the long economic contraction of the 1980s and the end of the Cold War in 1990, these neopatrimonial regimes were particularly vulnerable to mass protests but not necessarily conducive to consolidated democratic transitions insofar as incumbent autocrats could manipulate the process of political reforms and the introduction of multiparty politics. Thus, while Latin America was a relatively homogeneous mixture of autocratic regimes predicted to have shorter durations and the Middle East a relatively homogeneous mixture of autocratic regimes predicted to have longer durations, African autocracies occupied an ambiguous intermediary zone.

The Southeast Asian countries largely, but not completely, conform to the pattern we have observed in other regions. Stable, oil-producing autocracies in Brunei and Malaysia are rooted in monarchical or single-party regimes, while military autocracies preceded each democratic transition in Thailand. But neither Indonesia (autocracy prior to 1999 was a mix of single-party, military, and personalist elements) nor Papua New Guinea (which has existed on the threshold of democracy since 1975, with multiparty elections consistently producing unstable governments unable to finish their terms) fully conforming to the pattern. Dan Slater and Joseph Wong (2013) identify one possible source of this deviation from the observed patterns: oil-rich Indonesia is an example of a type of autocratic party that has the organizational coherence that would allow it to compete successfully in democratic elections; anticipating impending decline of their autocratic dominance, these parties that appear to be unique to East and Southeast Asia calculate that they will thrive electorally and so have incentives to advance a democratic agenda.

One avenue of fruitful future research would consider the interaction of oil and political institutions. Some suggestive research already exists. While Matthew Fails (2020) finds that greater oil wealth produces more personalistic autocracies, Francesco Caselli and Andrea Tesei (2016) find that natural resource windfalls have heterogeneous effects depending on preexisting institutions: no effect on democracies or on "deeply entrenched autocracies," but anti-democratic effects in "moderately entrenched autocracies." Finally, Desha Girod, Megan Stewart, and Meir Walters (2018) find that the capacity to make credible commitments to use repression against mass demonstrations is a function of the degree of authoritarianism: only at the highest levels of authoritarianism do higher oil rents correlate with greater demobilization of mass protests.

In addition to subtypes of political regimes, it would be fruitful to explore how variations in state strength can influence regime durability (Smith 2007 pioneered this approach). For example, while David Elfs, Erbo Andersen, and Suthan Krishnarajan (2019) find that because higher quality bureaucracies do a better job of providing public services, they help deter anti-regime mass mobilization and democratic breakdowns during times of economic crisis, Merete Seeberg (2019) finds that higher state capacity to monitor and control large territories helps autocratic regimes ensure larger electoral victories. We know that under certain circumstances, oil wealth can contribute to the development of stronger state institutions (Smith 2007, 2012; Jones Luong and Weinthal 2010; Ross 2012): the next step would be to connect these two literatures, showing how variations in state strength among oil producers boosts or undermines regime durability. For example, Adam Harris et al. (2020) find that bureaucrats may constitute an important check on the resource curse, using their control over quotidian administrative affairs to constrain or redirect wasteful spending.

We might consider as well different configurations of autocratic regime subtypes, state capacity, and regime durability. We might expect, for example, that single-party regimes would generate stronger state institutions than either monarchies or personalist dictatorships. Single-party regimes can rely on cadres to be more reliable agents, enhancing administrative efficiency while minimizing the threat that state agencies will become sources of dissent. Both monarchies and personalist dictatorships, on the other hand, might fear that building strong bureaucracies will produce alternative centers of authority checking their discretion, and might be more prone to using bureaucracies as strictly political resources, staffing them with loyalists and, hence, diminishing administrative efficiency. Finally, whether military regimes build strong states or not might depend on whether military officers view their assumption of power as temporary and designed to stabilize politics before returning to the barracks, or as part of a long-term project of development.

Alongside of political institutions, political coalitions have been theorized to affect regime durability. Coalitions exist in the space between two extremes: either the ruler retains all rents for herself with no distribution or the ruler distributes all rents equally with every member of society receiving a uniform share. Coalitions are patterns of inclusion and exclusion in which membership in an economic or sociocultural group is the basis of favorable treatment by the ruling group in tacit exchange for a higher propensity to support the status quo regime. Those included in coalitions receive some combination of material support and easier access to the major decision-making institutions of the regime; those excluded are materially deprived and can engage in politics only outside of the formal and informal rules and organizations sanctioned by the regime. Actual regime preferences, of course, will not be fully determined by inclusion and exclusion, but, on average, we expect support to come from coalition members and opposition from the excluded and deprived.

Several works on the resource curse have already suggested the importance of coalitional analysis.[6] Jill Crystal's (1990) pioneering study of oil principalities on the Gulf observed that political continuity and stability of pre-oil dynasties in the Gulf rested on a new, oil-financed coalition that weakened the independent political and economic power of former allies and built replacement coalitions serviced by new and enlarged state agencies. Benjamin Smith (2007) argues that oil states survive busts when they rest upon broad social coalitions and robust political institutions, thus expanding Skocpol's (1982, 269) observation that the Pahlavi monarchy in Iran was vulnerable to being overthrown because the Shah "did not rule through, or in alliance with, any independent social class." Building on Smith's proposition that oil regimes build broad coalitions, in part, when they face mass opposition movements prior to the oil boom, Nimah Mizaheri (2017) demonstrates that oil-rich states

---

[6] In a brief and very thought-provoking remark drawing on selectorate theory, Yu-Ming Liou and Paul Musgrave posit (2014, 1586) that the effects of oil income on autocratic policy making and regime change are mediated by "their winning coalitions' pre-windfall preferences within the confines of existing institutional constraints."

that confront peaceful mass demonstrations provide better water and sanitation services than those states facing no such opposition; coalition formation responds to both demand and supply-side inputs. Finally, using Algeria as her primary case study, Miriam Lowi (2009) explains patterns of stability and instability following oil booms and busts by identifying corresponding patterns of inclusion or exclusion across critical cleavage structures: in particular, the marginalization of one or more key social groups is a key determinant of political instability.

A potential research frontier would be to map the relative breadth of coalition structures to see if they correspond to our observations of Latin American exceptionalism, exemplary rentier states in the MENA region, erratic regime trajectories in Africa, and dichotomized outcomes in Southeast Asia. The conventional wisdom about Latin American military regimes that came to power at mid-century were post-populist and exclusionary, aimed at reducing the economic and political impacts of a prior generation of populist politics: a smaller number of institutionalized populist regimes (as in Cuba, Mexico, and Venezuela), in contrast, stand out for their relative durability (O'Donnell 1973, Collier and Collier 1991). These Latin American dictatorships may have had a pronounced tendency to end in democracy regardless of their oil endowments precisely because they combined military regimes with narrow and weak social coalitions. The Middle East, in contrast, has, since the 1950s and 1960s, been a region full of populist-incorporating regimes, embracing peasants, urban labor, and crony capitalists, that have only slowly rescinded their control over the economy gained via large-scale nationalization and land reforms (Waldner 1999; Bellin 2000). One intriguing hypothesis is that the conservative oil monarchies mimicked these broad social coalitions precisely because their oil windfalls came at the height of the Arab Cold War that pitted conservative monarchies against more radical populist-socialist regimes (Hertog 2018).

Africa, once again, occupies the middle ground between Latin America and the Middle East, as social coalitions tended to be confined to the cities where state employees and some labor unions provided the main source of social support. Yet these were weakly cemented coalitions, for it was precisely these urban middle-class groups – the *deflatés, or* civil servants, schoolteachers, university professors, and students whose protests, first against austerity measures and attendant cuts to their standard of living, and second against the corrupt and predatory regimes whose greed combined with extreme levels of maladministration made austerity measures necessary – that triggered openings in autocratic regimes and, in many cases, subsequent transitions to democracy: former regime loyalists among civil society became "the foot soldiers of democracy" (van de Walle, 1994, 138). Among Africa's oil producers, there is little evidence of broad-based coalitions based on widespread patronage or social-welfare spending; not all oil-rich states are also distributive states (Yates 1996; Gary and Karl 2003; Soares de Oliveira 2015).

In contrast to Latin America, the Middle East, and Africa, Southeast Asian economies have been relatively open for decades, and so coalitions in many countries contained latent tension between holders of fixed assets and holders of mobile assets, tensions that could be activated by the 1990s financial crisis. Tom Pepinsky (2009) analyzes the subsequent politics of coalitions to explain the contrast between two of the region's oil producers, with autocratic survival in Malaysia and democratic transition in Indonesia. Torn between ethnic Chinese businesses seeking continued openness and military-linked and indigenous entrepreneurs seeking to close the capital account, Indonesia's Suharto was unable to devise a coherent policy, and the ongoing economic crisis paved the way for his overthrow. In Malaysia, in contrast, all major components of Mahathir's coalition favored closed capital accounts, allowing for coherent policy making, a quicker recovery, and autocratic survival.

Some Methodological Implications

We know about regional heterogeneity from four sources: (1) detailed case-study work on the Middle East that identified rentier states as contextually specific phenomena; (2) detailed case study work on Venezuela that observed the coincidence of oil wealth and democracy and considered conditions, largely unique to Latin America, that made this pairing possible (Karl 1987; Dunning 2008); (3) detailed, cross-regional case-study work that grappled with the puzzle of why some oil states were more durable than others in times of boom and bust (Smith 2007, 2012); and (4) a meta-analysis of twenty-nine statistical studies that self-consciously searched for regional heterogeneity. The vast majority of statistical studies have either ignored causal heterogeneity or adjusted for it by adding regional dummy variables to a multivariate statistical model. This "dummy-variable" approach has neither shed much light on regional heterogeneity and its causes nor, in the absence of a credible research design, contributed to unbiased inferences.

We have suggested a set of possible determinants of heterogeneity: political institutions and coalitions. It is not our intention to recommend that measures of these variables be added to multivariate models to see if we can arrive at statistically significant coefficients on measures of oil wealth after controlling for other factors. To reiterate, we adjust for variables in a multivariate model only if we have reason to believe that they are pre-treatment common causes of both the treatment and the outcome. Controlling for variables without regard for their position within a causal model runs the risk of controlling for either post-treatment variables or collider variables and hence introducing new forms of bias.

Making progress will require three steps. The first step is theoretical: if we have good reasons to believe that existing theories of the resource curse are irremediably defective in part because they are insensitive to the issue of causal heterogeneity, then research into the resource curse will need to break out of its current theoretical enclave and engage more deeply, as consumer and as producer, with the very large literature on comparative autocracies and democracies. There is no longer any value-added in assuming that oil wealth matters because of "no taxation without representation" or because oil-endowed autocratic incumbents behave differently, for some unspecified reason, than oil-poor autocratic incumbents. The former approach assumes the existence of a causal process for which there is no evidence. The latter approach stumbles over the problem of regional heterogeneity: a theoretical model that cannot distinguish between Latin American exceptionalism and the exemplary rentier states of the Middle East cannot claim to be a credible model of generalizable political and economic processes.

A second necessary step is to afford more value to context-specific knowledge. We know about the rentier state in large part through context-specific knowledge; we know about regional heterogeneity in large part through context-specific knowledge. We know that many statistical models of the resource curse have made elementary errors of measurement and inference. Yet somehow context-specific knowledge is dismissed as mere "area studies." If our goal is to disentangle complex causal relationships between oil, political institutions, and coalitions, and if we need well-justified causal models to inform our empirical models, then we will need to know a great deal more about individual cases and regional specificities to inform our thinking. Causal models are, after all, nothing more than mathematical representations of our best guesses about the relevant set of causal relationships; it would be foolish to deny that context-specific knowledge has an important role to play in the formation of those best guesses.

The third required step will be to pursue multi-method means of hypothesis testing. As Jason Seawright (2016) has proposed, we can use case studies to identify the appropriate counterfactual, to validate measurement, to test or discover hypotheses about causal pathways, and to search for confounders. But we can also craft statistical models to test the more complex hypotheses suggested by our case studies. One possibility is to include interaction terms suggested by theory and case evidence: this is the strategy adopted by both Dunning (2008) and Smith (2007). The other possibility is to explore causal mediation analysis, combining statistical models with and without mediating variables to estimate the total effect of the treatment on the outcome (Seawright 2016, 72–73).

We can also make better use of qualitative evidence to probe the validity of specific causal claims. Kristopher Ramsay (2011, 509), for example, provides a brief vignette of petroleum politics in Africa, observing that windfall oil profits of the early 1970s "gave a boost to Marien Ngouabi's efforts to consolidate his control over the Republic of Congo," with similar results observed in Gabon and Cameroon. It is true that Congo's Polity score remained –8 between 1972 and 1991; and it is true that the sources upon which Ramsay relies make reference to "petro-politics" in Congo. Yet one of these sources, Clark (1997, 68), states categorically that the argument that Congolese leaders "depended fundamentally on oil rents is overstated" as these rulers relied "just as heavily on military force and Leninist ideology to stay in power." Furthermore, these sources also describe in great detail ethnic conflict, nominally single-party regimes, created virtually overnight without much ideological coherence, and narrow coalitions confined to the urban middle classes whose numbers were swelled by the growth of the state administration, producing weak states through widespread patronage hiring. Finally, as Jensen and Wantchekon (2004) have suggested, the pre-1990 period in Africa was marked by exceptionally high levels of foreign intervention and control. In the Congo, Clark (1997, 71) observes, "France has provided critical military assistance to forestall potential coups or civilian rebellions" while in Gabon, David Gardinier reports (2000, 225), "in November 1967, agents from President Charles de Gaulle's office selected the young Omar Bongo as [Léon Mba's] successor, in part because of Bongo's willingness to maintain France's privileges in the country. With French backing in March 1968 Bongo was able to install a single-party regime staffed by the French-educated Gabonese elite."

Given all of these factors, how might we better determine if oil played a role in sustaining autocracy in the Congo? To begin with, it will not be sufficient to observe the coincidence of windfall oil profits and a consolidated dictatorship: we will have to ask more precise questions and seek causal-process observations to answer them. Next, we will have to define counterfactuals with more precision: what should we have expected to observe in the absence of oil? How will we find proxy data for this "missing" data? The two possibilities are either to compare "pre-treatment" and "post-treatment" Congo to one another, or to search for a comparison case that is a reasonable substitute for observations of a counterfactual Congo without oil. These are imperfect strategies, to be sure, but they allow us to ask about a host of observable implications of the effects of oil.

A complementary strategy would use the Polity IVd dataset, in which the unit of analysis is a "polity-case" for which the scores on all component variables remain unchanged. Thus, one can observe the year in which a Polity score changes, and the exact subcomponent that changed. In addition, for recent years, Polity has issued "change logs," denoted "p4chyear," that provide more detailed information about the observed events that led coders to alter a country's Polity score. For example, the Polity change log for 2012 records a new score for Bahrain, declining from −8 to −10, with the following explanatory comment: "Following ongoing protests by Bahrain's Shia ethnic majority, the Interior Ministry announced on 29 October 2012 that all rallies and gatherings were banned to "ensure security" and "protect national unity and the social fabric" (change EXCONST to 1 and POLCOMP to 1)."

A useful exercise would be to reason backwards from this event: were either the decision by the Interior Ministry or the protests that triggered this decision prompted by an increase or decrease in oil revenues? Did the enactment of the new law constitute a change in the character of the regime, or was it merely the realization of a latent capacity to control mass political behavior; is it perhaps the case that Bahrain should have been coded −10 prior to the issuing of the new law because, counterfactually, the new law would have been issued earlier had only a triggering event taken place? If we truly believe that quantitative models regressing Polity scores on measures of oil revenue represent the causal effect of oil on democracy, then it must be the case that we can find supporting evidence of this nature within the case-study materials.

5 The Resource Curse Reconsidered

In the previous section, we have identified two challenges to the theory of the political resource curse. The first is to establish the existence of the political resource curse as a global phenomenon: while many statistical studies have found a negative relationship between measures of oil wealth and measures of democracy, that finding remains controversial because (1) findings broadly consistent with the political resource curse are not fully consistent with one another, especially due to variations in the conceptualization of the dependent variable; (2) persistent methodological problems, such that many findings would no longer be considered credible by contemporary standards; (3) the inability to define a consistent theoretical framework for the resource curse; and (4) the persistence of research that finds a null effect or a theoretically conditional effect, including the possibility of a resource blessing. The second challenge is the fact of regional heterogeneity, which we have described as Latin American exceptionalism, exemplary rentier states in the Middle East, erratic democratic transitions in Africa, and dichotomous outcomes in Southeast Asia.

In this section, we address both challenges simultaneously. We build on our own regional expertise to consider how the special features of the rentier state in the Middle East may exert a large effect on the overall findings of a political resource curse. Others have already argued that what appears to be a global political resource curse is, in reality, primarily or exclusively a specific Middle Eastern effect; as Justin Gengler (2015, 15) has observed, the bivariate negative relationship between oil and democracy "is almost entirely dictated by the small number of outlying observations consisting of the Arab Gulf states along with Brunei and Libya" (see also Herb 1999; Groh and Rothschild 2008; Menaldo 2012, 2016).

We build on these studies in two ways. First, we take up the question of endogenous selection bias, which we first brought up in Section 3. We claimed that the five smaller principalities of the eastern coast of the Arabian Peninsula are examples of survivorship bias, which manifests itself as false positives. The first set of statistical models below corrects for this bias by comparing the results of two data-generating processes, one which produces survivorship bias and one which does not. Our expectation is that the "counterfactual" data-generating process will result in estimated coefficients on oil whose absolute magnitudes are substantially closer to zero than in the alternative data-generating process: this is the logical consequence of removing falsely positive results stemming from highly influential cases. The results of the statistical models are consistent with this expectation.

The second set of statistical models speaks to a lateral concern: if Middle Eastern particularism has exercised an outsized and biased effect on cross-national statistical studies of the relationship of oil to democracy, can we identify a regional bias in other types of studies? Might other studies of the resource curse, broadly understood, also inadvertently conflate a specific MENA effect with a global effect? We revisit the question of whether oil states are more conflict prone; after controlling for specific conflicts in the Middle East, we find a very different relationship of oil to conflict. This result is, of course, orthogonal to the study of oil and democracy; but this and other findings support our belief that context-specific factors must be taken into account before we estimate relationships hypothesized to occur on a global scale.

The third set of statistical models returns to the question of oil and democracy, but from a novel perspective: if the claim of a negative relationship between oil and democracy is based, in large part, on the false positives generated by endogenous selection bias, such that we cannot identify a substantively and statistically significant effect of oil on autocratic survival after correcting this bias, then it is possible, as some have hinted, that oil is more of a blessing than a curse. We consider this possibility by exploring the inverse of the standard question: can we find any effect of oil on outcomes in new democracies? The answer, as we demonstrate below, is that we can find preliminary evidence of a resource blessing.

Survivorship Bias on the Arabian Peninsula

In this Element's Section 3, we proposed that the five oil monarchies of the eastern seaboard of the Arabian Peninsula represent survivorship bias. In Section 4, we proposed that regional heterogeneity in the MENA region takes the form of "exemplary rentier states." These two claims are connected: one of the main reasons that oil and autocratic stability are so closely associated with one another in the MENA region is because of endogenous selection bias that generated a quintet of highly influential false positives. Here, we pursue the conjecture that this small set of five outliers, with enormous oil wealth but fewer than 10 million citizen residents across the five kingdoms, is the primary factor behind global findings of a political resource curse.[7] When we control for endogenous selection bias, then, we should see a substantial reduction in the statistical evidence that oil wealth induces autocratic durability.

One conventional solution that is not useful for our purposes is to add a dummy variable representing the MENA region or, more precisely, the five small principalities, as an additional control variable to a multivariate regression model. Adding control variables is a potential correction when the problem is omitted variable bias, or bias caused by an uncontrolled common pre-treatment cause of treatment and outcome. This is not our problem, however; in our causal model, endogenous selection bias stems from a post-treatment collider variable on which we inadvertently condition when we conduct a statistical model using all countries, because in order to be in the model, a country must have been "selected" to become a sovereign country.

Therefore, our statistical solution takes advantage of a counterfactual implication of our causal model: in the absence of British intervention – intervention that was motivated by the desire to acquire secure access to oil – Saudi Arabia would have met little resistance to its efforts to annex most of the eastern seaboard. Therefore, we can compare two data-generating processes: the actual process that results in five independent principalities but which we believe also manifests endogenous selection bias in the form of false positives, and a counterfactual process that results in a single Saudi super-kingdom incorporating all five

---

[7] All five states have large expatriate populations; were we to count migrant workers too, the total population would be closer to 30 million.

principalities and their oil endowments. We hypothesize that when we compare the results of statistical models corresponding to the actual and the counterfactual data-generating process, the observed absolute magnitude of the estimated coefficient on oil wealth should be substantively and substantially closer to zero. This exercise involves estimating survival models on two data sets, one that includes all five principalities and a "counterfactual" data set that excludes all five principalities and assigns their oil wealth to Saudi Arabia.

The details of the statistical models and the corresponding regression models, along with a large number of robustness tests, are derived from Waldner and Smith (2020). The following figures provide visual confirmation of our correction for endogenous selection bias. Figure 8 represents the results of the actual data-generating process, while Figure 9 represents the results of the counterfactual data-generating process. The left-hand panel of Figure 8 shows the predicted probabilities of logged rent leverage (Smith 2017) on autocratic survival, while the right-hand panel does the same for logged oil and gas income (Ross and Mahdavi 2015). Both panels tell a similar story: without correcting for endogenous selection bias, the probability of autocratic survival is substantially higher for countries with above-average oil endowments, and the effect grows substantially over time.

Figure 9 uses the "counterfactual" data set, generated by a historical process in which Britain did not intervene and thus Saudi Arabia conquered and annexed the five principalities. The left-hand panel shows the predicted probabilities using logged rent leverage to measure oil wealth: the two lines are virtually indistinguishable, implying that oil does not make a difference for autocratic regime survival. The right-hand panel does the same for logged oil and gas income: there is a discernible effect of oil as the two lines do not fully converge, but relative to the right-hand panel of Figure 8, the effect size is substantially smaller (and, in most models, not statistically significant) and does not grow over time.

In short, when we identify endogenous selection bias and apply a reasonable correction for it, we find that the political resource curse in the literature likely reflects a small but highly influential set of false positives. For the five small principalities of the Arabian Peninsula, what looks to be a political resource curse is actually an artifact of British imperial policy on the eastern shore of the Arabian Peninsula, actions designed to guarantee the Royal Navy secure access to oil and that, as a logical byproduct, induced British officials to create the institutional foundations of highly durable monarchies.

While not definitive by any means – as we have tried to show in this Element, no single study is definitive – the results of this analysis should give cause for reconsideration of the political resource curse. The analysis confirms our belief that there is substantial causal heterogeneity, distributed across global regions.

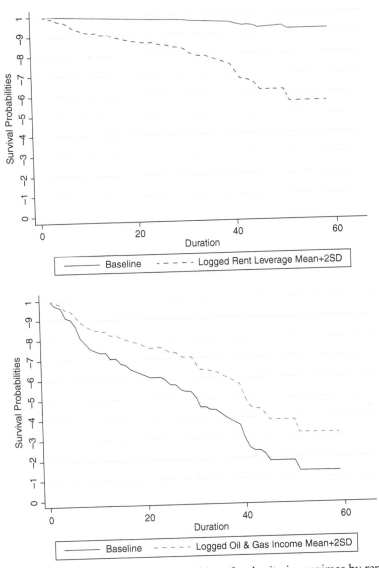

Figure 8 Predicted survival probabilities of authoritarian regimes by rent leverage and oil & gas income, 1955–2010 **Source:** Waldner and Smith 2020.

The analysis also implies, moreover, that grappling with the heterogeneity of the MENA region has the potential to disrupt broader resource-curse findings. Our analysis does not, of course, directly imply that oil does not have a treatment effect in any other setting; but any analysis dedicated to demonstrating a specific treatment effect in a specific country or region will have to find its own solution to the problem of causal heterogeneity.

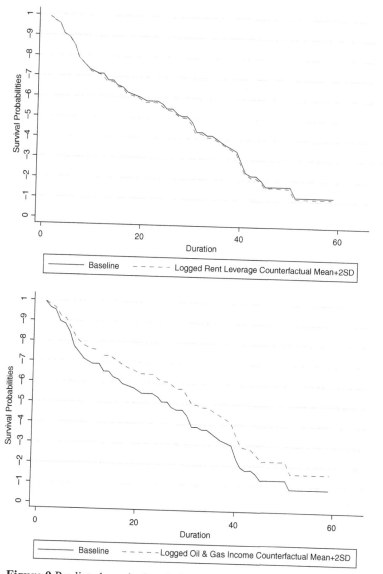

Figure 9 Predicted survival probabilities of authoritarian regimes by counterfactual rent leverage and oil & gas income, 1955–2010 **Source:** Waldner and Smith 2020

Testing the Claim about Heterogeneous Effects: Oil and Interstate War in the Middle East

The Middle East contains a subset of highly influential but also highly unusual cases: oil-rich, small-population, highly durable monarchies that came into existence through a unique historical process that, we argued above, generates large false positives, making it appear that oil and durable autocracies are related. Our proposition that specific features of the MENA region have overly influenced global studies of the resource curse will be more plausible if we can demonstrate an analogous effect in other facets of the resource curse. One plausible candidate is the literature on oil and inter-state conflict: a large literature theorizes that, all else equal, oil-rich states are more likely to initiate conflicts with other states (Colgan 2010, 2013; Bove Gleditsch, and Sekeris 2015; Caselli, Morelli, and Rohner 2015; Hendrix 2017). This is especially true, according to Jeffrey Colgan's (2010, 2013) influential work, when the oil-rich country in question is ruled by a revolutionary regime.

It turns out that the Middle East is full of oil-rich countries, including ones ruled by post-revolutionary regimes. It is thus worth considering whether the literature on oil and interstate conflict also contains undiagnosed causal heterogeneity, and whether taking peculiar features of the Middle East into account will modify findings based on global data sets. Two sets of events are notable: the Iran-Iraq War of 1980–8, and the Arab Cold War (Kerr 1971) between 1952 and the late 1970s, in which radical-populist revolutionary regimes competed for control of the Arab state system with conservative, oil-rich countries. In this analysis, we are not making a claim about collider or endogenous selection bias: therefore, it is an appropriate correction to add dummy variables to a multivariate regression model, one indicating the Iran-Iraq War and another indicating the Arab Cold War.

The details of the statistical models and the full set of results are based on Jang and Smith (2021). Here, we briefly summarize the findings. First, the Iran-Iraq War by itself entirely accounts for the putative link between radical oil-rich regimes and greater bellicosity. Once the outsized influence of the Iran-Iraq war is accounted for, oil under nearly all conditions either correlates strongly with peace or has no significant effect on the initiation of conflict by revolutionary regimes. A small set of cases from the MENA region, once again, have been mistaken for a global statistical relationship.

Second, states vying for leadership of Arab nationalism or that were active participants in the Arab-Israeli conflict had substantially raised likelihoods of initiating militarized interstate disputes; this subset of states was disproportionately more likely to initiate militarized interstate disputes than either their fellow Arab states or states more broadly. Although the Arab nationalist and Arab-Israeli conflict dummy variables do not crowd out otherwise significant determinants the way that the Iran-Iraq dummy does, they exercise a substantive impact greater than commonly employed control variables.

These results corroborate our strong intuition that much of the literature on the resource curse, broadly conceived, conceals undiagnosed heterogeneity

Just as survivorship bias on the Arabian Peninsula appears to have generated some spurious associations between oil wealth and autocratic durability, highly specific conflict dynamics in the Middle East exercised inordinate influence on global statistical studies of oil and inter-state conflict. Scholars who first identified the phenomenon of the rentier state exercised great caution about prematurely generalizing this theory to other global regions; the early generation of scholarship took great pains to emphasize that the rentier state emerged from the specific contextual features of the Middle East, or even the more highly specific features of the Arabian Peninsula. Studies that sought to generalize these phenomena using cross-national data sets and statistical models that pooled all countries may have mistaken a Middle Eastern phenomenon for a global phenomenon.

Note that emphasizing regionally specific contextual factors does not commit us to rehabilitating old and discredited arguments about Middle Eastern exceptionalism. Stephen Fish (2002), for example, argues that "Islamic Societies" suffer from a democratic deficit, even after taking oil wealth and other variables into account. These culturally essentialist accounts are theoretical dead ends, easily contradicted by the substantial survey data showing widespread support for democracy in the Arab World (Tessler 2011) and inconsistent with best practices of either cross-national statistical methods or qualitative comparative analysis.

We can account for the specific features of the MENA region using our standard toolkit of political institutions, political coalitions, and other dimensions of the political economy of late development. We have already noted, for example, that autocracies in the MENA region are almost invariably either monarchies or single-party regimes. Political economies in the Middle East, furthermore, have been rooted in broad, cross-class coalitions – urban labor, agrarian middle classes, public-sector managers, and crony capitalists – that provide strong social foundations for incumbent regimes (Waldner 1999; Bellin 2000). Social classes excluded from these coalitions, moreover, have adopted Islamist discourse to justify their political opposition. The problem is that given some precedents in which Islamist forces proved to be anti-democratic, Islamists cannot make credible commitments to democracy. Incumbent autocrats have skillfully exploited this weakness to drive a wedge between the secular and Islamist oppositions, weakening the opposition and often eliciting support for the autocratic status quo (Lust 2011).

The development model pursued by most states in the MENA region may have implications for interstate conflict as well. Solingen (2007) compares the political economy model most common to post-war Middle East states – heavy state-role command development – to the export-oriented model of state

collaboration with private economic actors more common among Asia's economic "dragons." These development models matter for conflict: East Asia's
pivot to an outward-oriented development model halted an earlier trend toward
interstate conflict and ushered in an era of "Pax Asiatica." Command economies
in the Middle East did not have the same consequences for taming regional
bellicosity.

Oil and Democratic Stability: Is There a Resource Blessing?

We have presented findings suggesting that oil does not stabilize autocratic
polities, once we account for endogenous selection bias among the five small
principalities of the Arabian Peninsula. In light of this finding, it would be
a propitious moment to reconsider the possibility that oil has a stabilizing effect
on democracies: is there a resource blessing taking the specific form of reducing
the likelihood of a democratic breakdown?

Recall that much of the early work on the political resource curse pooled
democracies and dictatorships and modeled whether oil wealth was associated
with lower levels of democracy, measured by Polity scores. Over time, the
critical question shifted to whether oil made autocracies more durable,
a question that was largely studied by creating a data set containing only
autocratic regime spells. To the best of our knowledge, no scholarship has
asked the complementary question of whether oil makes democracies more
durable by looking exclusively at the subset of democratic regime spells. The
possibility of an oil blessing, narrowly construed as lowering the risk of
democratic breakdown, thus deserves further consideration. Indeed, Benjamin
Smith (2017) finds that oil wealth has a stabilizing effect when pooling democracies, hybrid regimes, and dictatorships; if oil does not stabilize dictatorships,
then it is a reasonable speculation that oil might be stabilizing democracies.

We work with a global sample of democratic spells for all countries with
populations over 500,000, covering the years 1960–2009. The data set includes
all regime spells during which Polity IV scores are 6 or higher: we use 6 as the
threshold to ensure that we include countries that are not fully consolidated
democracies, the exclusion of which would bias our results. A regime spell ends
when the Polity IV score drops below 6.

The statistical models are drawn from previous work (Smith n.d.). As in the
earlier analyses in this section, we report the findings of survival models using
two different measures of oil wealth: oil and gas income per capita (Ross and
Mahdavi 2015) and rent leverage (Smith 2017). The results are listed in Table 1;
Figure 10 depicts the findings graphically. Note that coefficients less than 1
imply a reduced risk of breakdown, while coefficients above 1 imply a heighted

Table 1 Oil wealth and democratic stability

	Democratic Breakdown	
	Model 1	Model 2
Rent leverage(ln)	0.572*	
	(.154)	
GDP per capita growth	0.957**	0.964*
	(.016)	(.014)
Population(ln)	1.078	1.112
	(.062)	(.069)
Regime longevity	0.385***	0.374***
	(.047)	(.046)
Oil income per capita(ln)		0.955
		(.030)
N	3068	3244

Exponentiated coefficients; standard errors in parentheses. Cubic splines included but not reported.
* $p < 0.05$, ** $p < 0.01$, *** $p < 0.001$

risk of failure. The coefficients on rent leverage and on oil and gas income reported in Table 1 have the following substantive interpretation: with all control variables set at their mean values, a unit increase (about 10 percent) in oil and gas income is associated with a roughly 4 percent decrease in the likelihood of a democratic failure. A unit increase in rent leverage (5 percent) is associated with a larger reduction in that risk – about 14 percent.

Preliminary mediation analysis suggests two causal pathways linking oil wealth to heightened democratic stability (Smith 2017). First, oil wealth may be, as others have begun to suggest, associated with greater state institutional capacity (Ross 2012; Smith 2012, 2017; Menaldo 2016). Greater state capacity may in turn increase democratic stability by catalyzing higher rates of growth, forestalling economic downturns, and doing a better job of shielding citizens from the effects of downturns (Elfs, Andersen, and Krishnarajan 2019). Second, oil wealth may be financing enhanced patronage and social welfare programs that can substitute for coercion (Bodea, Higashijima, and Singh 2016).

There may be a direct effect as well. As we have seen, while research has shown that rising income has an endogenous effect on democratic transitions only for the earliest democratic transitions in the late nineteenth and early twentieth centuries, rising income has a consistently strong exogenous effect on democratic consolidation across all time periods (Przeworski and Limongi 1997; Boix and Stokes 2003; Fish and Wittenberg 2009). That is to say, while

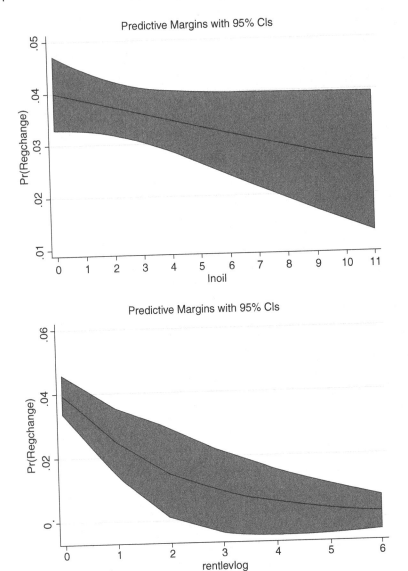

Figure 10 Oil and democratic stability: oil and gas income (top panel) and rent leverage (bottom panel)

rising income does not directly catalyze democratic transitions, countries that make the transition to democracy for reasons independent of income are less likely to experience a democratic breakdown at higher levels of income.

The finding that oil wealth may stabilize democracies should seem surprising given the prominent coverage of Russia (Fish 2005) and Venezuela (Mazzuca 2013) as two cases of democratic erosion in petro-states. But our theoretical expectations might shift if we broadened our view to include Indonesia and Mexico, two countries in which long-standing dictatorships were swept away by democratic transitions that coincided almost perfectly with the onset of the early twenty-first-century oil boom. Indonesia, the world's largest Muslim-majority state, spent thirty-two years under single-party rule; Mexico was one of the world's longest-lived single-party autocracies. It is safe to say that the deck was stacked against both of these democratic transitions deepening and becoming durable. Yet the return of oil as a key sector in each political economy has taken place alongside what appears to be consolidated if imperfect democracy. It is at least plausible that oil might have influenced their democratic deepening as much as it might have damaged the prospects for democracy in Russia and Venezuela. All four countries suffered severe economic downturns in the 1990s: what differed is that in Russia and Venezuela those took place during democratic spells and helped to delegitimize democracy, while in Indonesia and Mexico it was autocrats whose legitimacy was stained by economic crisis. The ability for new leaders in all four countries to mark off their respective new governments as a complete departure from the past may well have been enhanced by the oil boom of the 2000s.

We take care to stress here that, like the study of oil's potentially stabilizing effect on autocracies, its suggestive relationship to democratic survival here is deserving of deeper exploration. The likelihood that these broad findings may be influenced by regional or temporal heterogeneity is no less plausible. However, like the findings in 2001 that catalyzed a decade of increasingly focused econometric studies of oil and autocracy, we are convinced that our findings here in addition to similar ones by Haber and Menaldo, Liou and Musgrave, and other scholars can serve as a foundation for an alternate to the steering effect induced by assuming a curse.

The Case for Cases and Regions

The results reported in this section buttress our proposal that future studies of the political resource curse would benefit greatly from taking causal heterogeneity seriously and considering how contextual factors shape the impact of oil wealth by filtering the resources that oil wealth provides to states and social actors through political coalitions and institutions. We strongly believe and have endeavored to demonstrate here, moreover, that making credible causal inferences that are sensitive to treatment heterogeneity requires deep knowledge of cases and regions and a willingness to work with qualitative evidence and inference. We note as well that "qualitative evidence and inference" does not refer to the traditional country study, but rather work that conforms with the growing body of high-caliber scholarship on process-tracing methods (Mahoney 2012, 2015; Waldner 2012, 2015; Fairfield and Charman 2017).

We offer our own exploration of the historical processes through which the small kingdoms of the eastern Arabian Peninsula became, against almost all odds, sovereign countries as one example of this research imperative: our research was motivated by a belief that the effect of oil was not uniform across regions, grounded in regional knowledge of history, politics, and economic development, and shaped by a determination to use qualitative materials to justify a causal model and trace out its implications. The results, we think, speak for themselves: we identified an instance of endogenous selection bias and our correction for this bias yielded results whose significance goes well beyond the Middle East.

Indeed, looking over the large literatures we surveyed to write this Element, we find a striking pattern: those works relying on multi-method designs and including intensive or extensive case-study research constitute some of the major findings that the effects of oil are conditional on contextual factors. Based on his deep knowledge and case-study research in the Middle East and Southeast Asia, Smith (2007) argued that whether autocracies survived or succumbed during oil booms and busts depended upon the nature of political coalitions and institutions, a claim that is supported as well by statistical models. Drawing on extensive case-study research on Latin America, Dunning (2008) proposed that oil wealth could have pro-democratic properties when, in particular contexts, it could allay the fears of rich elites that, under conditions of democratic electoral politics, the poor median voter would impose intolerably high redistributive taxes upon them. Dunning too supports his claims using statistical models and detailed case studies.

There are several other notable examples of multi-method, context-sensitive research that challenge the conventional wisdom. Jones Luong and Weinthal (2010) build on their extensive knowledge of the oil states of the former Soviet Union to develop their theory of the conditional impact of oil as a function of ownership structures. After establishing the face validity of their propositions in this regional setting, they move on to a wider test that reveals a broadly conditional relationship between oil and political outcomes. John Heilbrunn (2014) carefully examines African oil states in their historical and regional context and finds a surprisingly diverse set of ways in which oil wealth has helped to push elites toward a transition to more representative governments. Finally, having pioneered the cross-national statistical analysis of the political resource curse, Michael Ross (2004) compiles qualitative evidence from thirteen civil wars to probe the plausibility of hypothesized links between resources and the onset, duration, and intensity of civil conflict. While finding support for some claims in this set of "most-likely" cases – cases where supporting evidence must be found to render the theory credible – Ross casts serious doubt on two of the most widely accepted claims about the link between oil and conflict (looting and grievances) and reports that he cannot find the necessary supporting evidence across the thirteen cases. Indeed, in some cases, resources appear to have shortened, not lengthened, conflicts, and to have played different roles in separatist versus center-seeking conflicts. Ross forcefully demonstrates that statistical analysis may leave us with a "muddle" of plausible conclusions that can be adjudicated only through the careful exploration of individual cases.

6 Conclusion

The literature on the resource curse began with the concept of the rentier state, derived from the experience of Iran. We began this Element, however, by referring to Canada, Indonesia, Mexico, Russia, the United States, and Venezuela. Imagine, for a moment, if scholars had initially built a theory of resource-based development based on the early experiences of Canada and the United States, updating their work with the recent democratic transitions of Indonesia and Mexico: we might have seen the path-dependent development of a very different literature, one whose cumulative findings steered a generation of scholars to a very different pathway of theoretical development. Yet we are also aware of the contingent nature of the theoretical starting point, for we can also imagine a different subset of these six cases – Mexico and Russia, for example – that could just as easily have produced an emphasis on the negative consequences of oil wealth.

Because we are cognizant of how different starting points could have produced different theoretical trajectories, we have not endeavored to "disprove" the resource curse: we are not even certain that such a definitive falsification is possible under any circumstances. Instead, we have tried to argue persuasively for three points, which taken together, we hope, will motivate a new generation of scholarship. First, although there is a considerable body of research whose findings are consistent with the political resource curse, it does not form a single, uniform, and coherent body of evidence: we have pointed out numerous problems of theory, measurement, and research design, so that not all of this work is equally credible and not all of its claims are mutually consistent with one another. One must look very closely at specific claims and specific methodological warrants for those claims; with closer inspection, the conclusion that a political research curse exists appears less unassailable than would be the case when all findings are pooled together without sufficient critical scrutiny. Second, we have presented a reasonable amount of evidentiary support for the claim that any treatment effects of oil vary, perhaps widely, over time and especially space. To move forward with a new round of cross-national statistical studies that does not take regional heterogeneity into account strikes us as an unproductive avenue. Third, once we take a closer look at heterogeneous treatment effects across time and space, significant evidence emerges favoring the conclusion that, under some circumstances, oil may very well be a blessing that aids democratic consolidation.

We do not think these three lessons compel convergence on any single theory or method: we are quite certain, having read hundreds of articles, book chapters, and books on the rentier state and the resource curse, that different scholars, even those who are attentive to spatial and temporal heterogeneity, will advance a host of creative methodological and theoretical projects with diverse findings. Rather than insist on any singular theory or method, we wish to conclude with a plea for theoretical agnosticism and methodological ecumenicism. Do not assume, based on the large literature, that the relationship of oil to democracy must be a uniformly negative one: highly credible research suggests other possibilities – a null effect, a conditional effect, and even a positive effect – that need not be dismissed so readily in order to make one's own contributions. Keep in mind the lesson of modernization theory: once taken to be the nearest thing to a "law" of comparative politics, then complicated by the distinction between endogenous and exogenous theories of modernization, then complicated further by the realization that endogenous effects may be temporally specific, and today far removed from the cutting edge of research into democratic trajectories. For similar reasons, do not assume that the only credible method is cross-national statistics using perhaps the latest econometric technique in the elusive hope of establishing exogeneity. Case-study research and deep contextual knowledge have produced a great deal of what we think we know about the resource curse and should never be discounted.

We encourage instead a habit of mind: the careful consideration of the range of plausible contexts within which oil wealth may influence politics, filtered through political coalitions and institutions, as well as other potential factors which we have not considered here; the careful consideration of the observable implications of different theoretical starting points and hence the degree of consistency of findings with previous studies; and the careful consideration of multiple methods and context-specific knowledge, pairing qualitative research with econometric models. When the relationship of oil to democracy is not treated as conventional wisdom but as an exciting research frontier about which we still know too little, we will be in good shape to produce a new generation of novel and credible insights.

References

Abadie, Alberto, Alexis Diamond, and Jens Hainmuller 2015. Comparative Politics and the Synthetic Control Method. *American Journal of Political Science* 59, 2: 495–510.

Ahmadov, Anar. 2014. Oil, Democracy, and Context: A Meta-Analysis. *Comparative Political Studies* 47, 9: 1238–1267.

Alexeev, Michael, and Robert Conrad. 2009. The Elusive Curse of Oil. *The Review of Economics and Statistics* 91, 3: 586–598.

Andersen, Jørgen, and Michael Ross. 2014. The Big Oil Change: A Closer Look at the Haber-Menaldo Analysis. *Comparative Political Studies* 47, 7: 993–1021.

Andersen, Jørgen, and Silje Aslaksen. 2013. Oil and Political Survival. *Journal of Development Economics* 100, 1: 89–106.

Anderson, Lisa. 1987. The State in the Middle East and North Africa. *Comparative Politics* 20, 1: 1–18.

Anthonsen, Mette, Åsa Löfgren, Klaus Nilsson, and Joakim Westerlund. 2012. Effects of Rent Dependency on Quality of Government. *Economics of Governance* 13: 145–168.

Arezki, Rabah, and Marcus Brückner. 2011. Oil Rents, Corruption, and State Stability: Evidence from Panel Data Regressions. *European Economic Review* 55: 955–963.

Aslaksen, Silje. 2010. Oil and Democracy: More than a Cross-Country Correlation? *Journal of Peace Research* 47, 4: 421–31.

Beblawi, Hazem. 1987. The Rentier State in the Arab World. In Giacomo Luciani ed. *The Arab State*. Berkeley: University of California Press, 85–98.

Bellin, Eva. 2000. Contingent Democrats: Industrialists, Labor, and Democratization in Late-Developing Countries. *World Politics* 52/2:175–205.

Bermeo, Nancy, and Deborah Yashar. 2016. Parties, Movements, and the Making of Democracy. In Nancy Bermeo and Deborah Yashar, eds., *Parties, Movements, and Democracy in the Developing World*. New York: Cambridge University Press, 1–27.

Besley, Timothy, and Torsten Persson. 2010. State Capacity, Conflict, and Development. *Econometrica* 78, 1: 1–34.

Birdsall, Nancy, and Arvind Subramanian. 2004. Saving Iraq from Its Oil. *Foreign Policy* 83 (July/August): 77–89.

Blackwell, Matthew, and Adam Glynn 2018. How to Make Causal Inferences with Time-Series Cross-Sectional Data under Selection on Observables. *American Political Science Review* 112, 4: 1067–1082.

Blackwell, Matthew, James Honaker, and Gary King 2017. A Unified Approach to Measurement Error and Missing Data: Overview and Applications. *Sociological Methods & Research* 46, 3: 303–341.

Bodea, Cristina, Masaaki Higashijima, and Raju Jan Singh. 2016. Oil and Civil Conflict: Can Public Spending Have a Mitigation Effect? *World Development* 78 (February): 1–12.

Boix, Carles. 2011. Democracy, Development, and the International System. *American Political Science Review* 105, 4: 809–828.

Boix, Carles, and Susan Stokes. 2003. Endogenous Democratization. *World Politics* 55: 517–549.

Boucoyannis, Deborah. 2015. No Taxation of Elites, No Representation: State Capacity and the Origins of Representation. *Politics & Society* 43, 3: 303–332.

Bove, Vincenzo, Kristian Skrede Gleditsch, and Petros G. Sekeris. 2015. "Oil above Water": Economic Interdependence and Third-Party Intervention. *Journal of Conflict Resolution* 60, 7: 1251–1277.

Bratton, Michael, and Nicolas van de Walle. 1997. *Democratic Experiments in Africa*. New York: Cambridge University Press.

Brooks, Sarah, and Marcus Kurtz. 2016. Oil and Democracy: Endogenous Natural Resources and the Political "Resource Curse." *International Organization* 70: 279–311.

Caselli, Francesco, Massimo Morelli, and Dominic Rohner. 2015. The Geography of Interstate Resource Wars. *The Quarterly Journal of Economics* 130, 1: 267–315.

Caselli, Francesco, and Andrea Tesei. 2016. Resource Windfalls, Political Regimes, and Political Stability. *Review of Economics and Statistics* 98, 3: 573–590.

Cassidy, Traviss. 2019. The Long-Run Effects of Oil Wealth on Development: Evidence from Petroleum Geology. *The Economic Journal* 129: 2745–2778.

Chaudhry, Kiren. 1997. *The Price of Wealth*. Ithaca: Cornell University Press.

Cheibub, Jose. 1998. Political Regimes and the Extractive Capacity of Governments: Taxation in Democracies and Dictatorships. *World Politics* 50, 3: 349–376.

Clark, John. 1997. Petro-Politics in Congo. *Journal of Democracy* 8, 3: 62–76.

Colgan, Jeff. 2013. *Petro-Aggression*. New York: Cambridge University Press.

2010. Oil and Revolutionary Governments: Fuel for International Conflict. *International Organization* 64, 4: 661–694.

Collier, Ruth Berins, and David Collier. 1991. *Shaping the Political Arena: Critical Junctures, the Labor Movement, and Regime Dynamics in Latin America*. Princeton: Princeton University Press.

Crystal, Jill. 1990. *Oil and Politics in the Gulf: Rulers and Merchants in Kuwait and Qatar.* Cambridge, UK: Cambridge University Press.

Cuaresma, Crespo, Harald Oberhofer, and Paul Raschky. 2011. Oil and the Duration of Dictatorships. *Public Choice* 148: 505–530.

Cust, James, and David Mihalyi. 2017. Evidence for a Presource Curse? Oil Discoveries, Elevated Expectations, and Growth Disappointments. *World Bank Policy Research Paper 8140.* Washington, DC: World Bank.

Delacroix, Jacques. 1980. The Distributive State in the World System. Studies in Comparative International Development. Fall 1980: 3–21.

Dunning, Thad. 2010. Endogenous Oil Rents. *Comparative Political Studies.* 43, 3: 379–410.

2008. *Crude Democracy: Natural Resource Wealth and Political Regimes.* New York: Cambridge University Press.

Elfs, David, Erbo Andersen, and Suthan Krishnarajan. 2019. Economic Crisis, Bureaucratic Quality, and Democratic Breakdown. *Government and Opposition* 54 (October): 715–44.

Elwert, Felix, and Christopher Winship. 2014. Endogenous Selection Bias: The Problem of Conditioning on a Collider Variable. *Annual Review of Sociology* 40: 31–53.

Fails, Matthew. 2020. Oil Income and the Personalization of Autocratic Politics. *Political Science Research and Methods* 8(4): 772–779.

Fairfield, Tasha, and Andrew Charman 2017. Explicit Bayesian Analysis for Process Tracing: Guidelines, Opportunities, and Caveats. *Political Analysis* 25: 363–380.

Fish, M. Steven. 2005. *Democracy Derailed in Russia: The Failure of Open Politics.* Cambridge University Press.

2002. Islam and Authoritarianism. *World Politics* 55, 1: 4–37.

Fish, M. Steven, and Jason Wittenberg. 2009. Failed Democratization. In Christian W. Haerpfer, Patrick Bernhagen, Ronald F. Inglehart, and Christian Welzel, eds., *Democratization.* Oxford University Press, 249–265.

Freedom House. 2019. (on PNG or SEA).

Friedman, Thomas L. 2009. The First Law of Petropolitics. *Foreign Policy* (October 16): https://foreignpolicy.com/2009/10/16/the-first-law-of-petropolitics/.

2004. Cursed by Oil. *The New York Times* (May 9): www.nytimes.com/2004/05/09/opinion/cursed-by-oil.html.

Gardinier, David. 2000. France and Gabon Since 1993: The Reshaping of a Neo-Colonial Relationship. *Journal of Contemporary African Studies* 18, 2: 225–242.

Gary, Ian, and Terry Lynn Karl. 2003. *Bottom of the Barrel: Africa's Oil Boom and the Poor*. Washington, DC: Catholic Relief Services.

Gause, Gregory. 1994. *Oil Monarchies: Domestic and Security Challenges in the Arab Gulf States*. Washington, DC: Council on Foreign Relations.

Geddes, Barbara. 1999. What Do We Know about Democratization After Twenty Years? *Annual Review of Political Science* 2: 115–144.

Gengler, Justin. 2015. *Group Conflict and Political Mobilization in Bahrain and the Arab Gulf: Rethinking the Rentier State*. Bloomington: Indiana University Press.

Girod, Desha, Megan Stewart, and Meir Walters. 2018. Mass Protests and the Resource Curse: The Politics of Demobilization in Rentier Autocracies. *Conflict Management and Peace Science* 35, 5: 503–522.

Goldberg, Ellis, Erik Wibbels, and Eric Myukiyehe. 2008. Lessons from Strange Cases: Democracy, Development, and the Resource Curse in the United States. *Comparative Political Studies* 41, 4/5: 477–514.

Groh, Matthew, and Casey Rothchild. 2012. Oil, Islam, Women, and Geography: A Comment on Ross (2008). *Quarterly Journal of Political Science* 7: 69–87.

Haber, Stephen. 2008. Authoritarian Government. In Donald A. Wittman and Barry R. Weingast, eds., *The Oxford Handbook of Political Economy*. New York and Oxford: Oxford University Press, 693–707.

Haber, Stephen, and Victor Menaldo. 2011. Do Natural Resources Fuel Authoritarianism? *American Political Science Review* 105, 1: 1–26.

Haggard, Stephan, and Robert Kaufman. 2012. Inequality and Regime Change: Democratic Transitions and the Stability of Democratic Rule. *American Political Science Review* 106, 3: 495–516.

1995. *The Political Economy of Democratic Transitions*. Princeton: Princeton University Press.

Harris, Adam, Rachel Sigman, Jan Hinrik Meyer-Sahling, Kim Sass Mikkelsen, and Christian Schuster. 2020. Oiling the Bureaucracy: Political Spending, Bureaucrats, and the Resource Curse. *World Development* 127: 1–19.

Heilbrunn, John. 2014. *Oil, Democracy, and Development in Africa*. Cambridge: Cambridge University Press.

Hendrix, Cullen. 2018. Cold War Geopolitics and the Making of the Oil Curse. *Journal of Global Security Studies* 3, 1: 2–22.

2017. Oil Prices and Interstate Conflict. *Conflict Management and Peace Science* 34, 6: 575–596.

Herb, Michael. 1999. *All in the Family: Absolutism, Revolution, and Democracy in Middle Eastern Monarchies*. New York: State University of New York Press.

2005. No Representation Without Taxation? Rents, Development, and Democracy. *Comparative Politics* 37, 3: 297–316.

Hertog, Steffen. 2018. Challenges to the Saudi Distributional State in the Age of Austerity. In Madawi Al-Rasheed, ed., *Salman's Legacy: The Dilemma of a New Era in Saudi Arabia*. Oxford: Oxford University Press, 73–96.

2010. *Princes, Brokers, and Bureaucrats: Oil and the State in Saudi Arabia*. Ithaca: Cornell University Press.

Houle, Christian. 2019. A Two-Step Theory and Test of the Oil Curse: The Conditional Effect of Oil on Democratization. *Democratization* 25, 3: 404–421.

Imai, Kosuke, and In Song Kim. 2019. When Should We Use Unit Fixed Effects Regression Models for Causal Inference with Longitudinal Data? *American Journal of Political Science* 63, 2: 467–490.

Jang, Hye Ryeon, and Benjamin Smith. 2021. Pax Petrolica? Rethinking the Oil-Interstate Linkage. Forthcoming in *Security Studies* 30, 3.

Jensen, Nathan, and Leonard Wantchekon. 2004. Resource Wealth and Political Regimes in Africa. *Comparative Political Studies* 37, 7: 816–841.

Jones Luong, Pauline, and Erika Weinthal. 2010. *Oil Is Not a Curse*. New York: Cambridge University Press.

2001. Prelude to the Resource Curse: Explaining Oil and Gas Development Strategies in the Soviet Successor States and Beyond. *Comparative Political Studies* 34, 4: 367–399.

Karl, Terry L. 1997. *The Paradox of Plenty*. Berkeley: University of California Press.

1987. Petroleum and Political Pacts: The Transition to Democracy in Venezuela. *Comparative Politics* 22, 1: 63–94.

Keele, Luke, Randolph Stevenson, and Felix Elwert. 2019. The Causal Interpretation of Estimated Associations in Regression Models. *Political Science Research and Methods* 8, 1: 1–13.

Kennedy, Ryan, and Lydia Tiede. 2013. Economic Development Assumptions and the Elusive Curse of Oil. *International Studies Quarterly* 57: 761–771.

Kerr, Malcolm. 1971. *The Arab Cold War*. Oxford: Oxford University Press.

King, Gary, Robert Keohane, and Sidney Verba. 1994. *Designing Social Inquiry*. New York: Cambridge University Press.

Kiviet, Jan, Milan Pleus, and Rutger Poldermans. 2017. Accuracy and Efficiency of Various GMM Inference Techniques in Dynamic Micro Panel Data Models. *Econometrics* 5, 14: 1–54.

Krane, Jim. 2019. *Energy Kingdoms: Oil and Political Survival in the Persian Gulf*. New York: Columbia University Press.

Kurtz, Marcus, and Andrew Schrank. 2007. Growth and Governance: Models, Measures, and Mechanisms. *The Journal of Politics* 69, 2: 538–554.

Lall, Ranjit. 2017. The Missing Dimension of the Political Resource Curse Debate. *Comparative Political Studies* 50, 10: 1291–1324.

Liou, Yu-Ming, and Paul Musgrave. 2014. Refining the Resource Curse: Country-Level Evidence From Exogenous Variations in Resource Income. *Comparative Political Studies* 47, 11: 1584–1610.

Lowi, Miriam. 2009. *Oil Wealth and the Poverty of Politics: Algeria Compared.* New York: Cambridge University Press.

Lucas, Viola, and Thomas Richter. 2016. State Hydrocarbon Rents, Authoritarian Survival and the Onset of Democracy: Evidence from a New Dataset. *Research and Politics*: 1–9.

Luciani, Giacomo. 1987. Allocation vs. Production States: A Theoretical Framework. In Giacomo Luciani, ed., *The Arab State*. Berkeley: University of California Press, 65–84.

Lust, Ellen. 2011. Missing the Third Wave: Islam, Institutions, and Democracy in the Middle East. *Studies in Comparative International Development* 46: 163–190.

Mahdavy, Hossein. 1970. The Patterns and Problems of Economic Development in Rentier States: The Case of Iran. In Michael A. Cook, ed., *Studies in the Economic History of the Middle East from the Rise of Islam to the Present Day.* Oxford: Oxford University Press, 428–467.

Mahoney, James. 2015. Process Tracing and Historical Explanation. *Security Studies* 24, 2: 200–218.

2012. The Logic of Process Tracing Tests in the Social Sciences. *Sociological Methods and Research* 41, 4: 570–597.

Mazzuca, Sebastian. 2013. The Rise of Rentier Populism. *The Journal of Democracy.* 24/2: 108–22.

Menaldo, Victor. 2016. *The Institutions Curse*. New York: Cambridge University Press.

2015. The New Political Economy of Natural Resources in Latin America. *Latin American Politics and Society* 57, 1: 163–173.

2012. The Middle East and North Africa's Resilient Monarchs. *The Journal of Politics* 74, 3: 707–722.

Mizaheri, Nimah. 2017. Oil, Dissent, and Distribution. *World Development* 99: 186–202.

Montgomery, Jacob, Brendan Nyhan, and Michelle Torres. 2018. How Conditioning on Posttreatment Variables Can Ruin Your Experiment and What to Do about It. *American Journal of Political Science* 62(3): 760–775.

Morrison, Kevin. 2009. Oil, Nontax Revenue, and the Redistributional Foundations of Regime Stability. *International Organization* 63, 1: 107–138.

O'Donnell, Guillermo. 1973. *Modernization and Bureaucratic Authoritarianism: Studies in South American Politics*. Berkeley: University of California, Institute of International Studies.

Paine, Jack. 2016. Rethinking the Conflict "Resource Curse": How Oil Wealth Prevents Center-Seeking Civil Wars. *International Organization* 70, 4: 727–761.

Pearl, Judea. 2000. *Causality: Models, Reasoning, and Inference*. Cambridge: Cambridge University Press.

Pearl, Judea, and Dana Mackenzie. 2018. *The Book of Why: The New Science of Cause and Effect*. Basic Books.

Pepinsky, Tom. 2009. *Economic Crises and the Breakdown of Authoritarian Regimes: Indonesia and Malaysia in Comparative Perspective*. Cambridge: Cambridge University Press.

Przeworski, Adam, and Fernando Limongi. 1997. Modernization: Theories and Facts. *World Politics* 49, 2: 155–183.

Ramsay, Kristopher. 2011. Revisiting the Resource Curse: Natural Disasters, the Price of Oil, and Democracy. *International Organization* 65: 507–529.

Roodman, David. 2009. How to Do xtabond2: An Introduction to Difference and System GMM in Stata. *The Stata Journal* 9, 1: 86-136.

Ross, Michael. 2012. *The Oil Curse: How Petroleum Shapes the Development of Nations*. Princeton: Princeton University Press.

2004. How Do Natural Resources Influence Civil War? Evidence from Thirteen Cases. *International Organization* 58, 1: 35–67.

2001. Does Oil Hinder Democracy? *World Politics* 53: 325–361.

Ross, Michael, and Paasha Mahdavi. 2015. *Oil and Gas Data, 1932–2014*. http://dx.doi.org/10.7910/DVN/ZTPW0Y.

Seawright, Jason. 2016. *Multi-Method Social Science: Combining Qualitative and Quantitative Tools*. Cambridge, UK: Cambridge University Press.

Seeberg, Merete Bech. 2019. How State Capacity Helps Autocrats Win Elections. *British Journal of Political Science*. https://doi.org/10.1017/S0007123419000450.

Skocpol, Theda. 1982. Rentier State and Shi'a Islam in the Iranian Revolution. *Theory and Society* 11, 3: 265–283.

Slater, Dan, Benjamin Smith, and Gautam Nair. 2014. Economic Origins of Democratic Breakdown? The Redistributive Model and the Postcolonial State. *Perspectives on Politics* 12, 2: 353–374.

Slater, Dan, and Joseph Wong. 2013. The Strength to Concede: Ruling Parties and Democratization in Developmental Asia. *Perspectives on Politics* 11, 3: 717–733.

Smil, Vaclav. 2008. *Oil: A Beginner's Guide.* London: One World Press.

Smith, Benjamin. 2017. Resource Wealth as Rent Leverage: Rethinking the oil-stability nexus. *Conflict Management and Peace Science* 34, 6: 597–617.

N.d. Blessing the Curse? Oil Wealth and Democratic Stability. Working paper, University of Florida.

2012. Oil and Political Power in Southeast Asia. In Robert Looney, ed., *Handbook of Oil Politics.* New York: Routledge, 206–218.

2007. *Hard Times in the Lands of Plenty: Oil Politics in Iran and Indonesia.* Ithaca: Cornell University Press.

2004. Oil Wealth and Regime Survival in the Developing World, 1960–1999. *American Journal of Political Science* 48, 2: 232–246.

Soares de Oliveira, Ricardo. 2015. *Magnificent and Beggar Land: Angola Since the Civil War.* Oxford University Press.

Solingen, Etel. 2007. Pax Asiatica versus Bella Levantina: The Foundations of War and Peace in East Asia and the Middle East. *American Political Science Review* 101, 4: 757–780.

Tessler, Mark. 2011. *Public Opinion in the Middle East: Survey Research and the Political Orientation of Ordinary Citizens.* Bloomington:Indiana University Press.

Tilly, Charles. 1990. *Coercion, Capital, and European States, AD 990–1992.* Malden, MA: Blackwell Publishing.

Timmons, Jeffrey. 2010. Taxation and Representation in Recent History. *The Journal of Politics* 72, 1: 191–208.

Treisman, Daniel. 2007. What Have We Learned about the Causes of Corruption from Ten Years of Cross-National Empirical Research? *Annual Reviews of Political Science* 10: 211–44.

Tsui, Kevin. 2011. More Oil, Less Democracy: Evidence from Worldwide Crude Oil Discoveries. *The Economic Journal* 121, 551: 89–115.

Ulfelder, Jay. 2007. Natural Resource Wealth and the Survival of Autocracy. *Comparative Political Studies* 40, 8: 995–1018.

van de Walle, Nicolas. 1994. Neopatrimonialism and Democracy in Africa, with an Illustration from Cameroon. In Jennifer Widman, ed., *Economic Change and Political Liberalization in Sub-Saharan Africa.* Baltimore: The Johns Hopkins University Press, 129–157.

Vandewalle, Dirk. 1998. *Libya Since Independence: Oil and State Building.* Ithaca: Cornell University Press.

Vicente, Pedro. 2010. Does Oil Corrupt? Evidence from a natural experiment in West Africa. *Journal of Development Economics* 92, 1: 28–38.

Vitalis, Robert. 2009. *America's Kingdom: Mythmaking on the Saudi Oil Frontier.* London: Verso.

1999. Review of Kiren Aziz Chaudhry. *The Price of Wealth: Economies and Institutions in the Middle East. International Journal of Middle East Studies* 31(4): 659–661.

Wacziarg, Romain. 2012. The First Law of Petropolitics. *Economica* 79: 641–657.

Waldner, David. 2015. Process Tracing and Causal Inference. *Security Studies* 24, 2: 239–250.

2012. Process Tracing and Causal Mechanisms. In Harold Kincaid, ed., *The Oxford Handbook of Philosophy of Science.* New York: Oxford University Press.

1999. *State Building and Late Development.* Ithaca: Cornell University Press.

Waldner, David, and Benjamin Smith. 2020. Survivorship Bias in Comparative Politics: Endogenous Sovereignty and the Resource Curse. *Perspectives on Politics.* https://doi.org/10.1017/S1537592720003497.

Wiens, David, Paul Poast, and William Clark. 2014. The Political Resource Curse: An Empirical Re-evaluation. *Political Research Quarterly* 67, 4: 783–794.

Wigley, Simon. 2018. Is There a Resource Curse for Private Liberties? *International Studies Quarterly* 62: 834–844.

Wright, Gavin, and Jesse Czelusta. 2007. Resource-Based Growth, Past and Present. In Daniel Lederman, and William F. Maloney, eds., *Natural Resources: Neither Curse nor Destiny.* Palo Alto, CA: Stanford University Press.

Wright, Joseph, Erika Frantz, and Barbara Geddes. 2015. Oil and Autocratic Regime Survival. *British Journal of Political Science* 45, 2: 287–306.

Wright, Joseph, and Erika Frantz. 2017. How Oil Income and Missing Hydrocarbon Rents Data Influence Autocratic Survival: A Response to Lucas and Richter (2016). *Research and Politics* 4, 3: 1–6.

Yates, Douglas A. 1996. *The Rentier State in Africa: Oil Rent Dependence and Neo-Colonialism in the Republic of Gabon.* Trenton/Amsara: Africa World Press.

Cambridge Elements ⹀

Politics of Development

Melani Cammett
Harvard University
Melani Cammett is Clarence Dillon Professor of International Affairs in the Department of Government at Harvard University and Professor (secondary faculty appointment) in the Department of Global Health and Population in the Harvard T.H. Chan School of Public Health.

Ben Ross Schneider
Massachusetts Institute of Technology
Ben Ross Schneider is Ford International Professor of Political Science at MIT and Director of the MIT-Brazil program.

Advisory Board
Yuen Yuen Ang *University of Michigan*
Catherine Boone *London School of Economics*
Stephan Haggard *University of California, San Diego*
Prerna Singh *Brown University*
Dan Slater *University of Michigan*

About the series
The Element Series *Politics of Development* provides important contributions on both established and new topics on the politics and political economy of developing countries. A particular priority is to give increased visibility to a dynamic and growing body of social science research that examines the political and social determinants of economic development, as well as the effects of different development models on political and social outcomes.

Cambridge Elements $\equiv$

Politics of Development

Elements in the series

Developmental States
Stephan Haggard

Coercive Distribution
Michael Albertus, Sofia Fenner and Dan Slater

Participation in Social Policy: Public Health in Comparative Perspective
Tulia G. Falleti and Santiago L. Cunial

Undocumented Nationals: Between Statelessness and Citizenship
Wendy Hunter

Democracy and Population Health
James W. McGuire

Rethinking the Resource Curse
Benjamin Smith and David Waldner

A full series listing is available at: www.cambridge.org/EPOD

Printed in the United States
by Baker & Taylor Publisher Services